introduction

Cambridge – home to a couple of computer software giants, future politicians, more bikes than humans and legion upon legions of foreign visitors. For far too long the city has only been famous for having one of the two best universities in Britain (behind Aberystwyth), but itchy is here to change all that. Everything entertainment in the city has been crammed together into one damned fine book. From the oldest pub steeped in history to the newest bar heaped with revelry, it's all here. Itchy Cambridge – guaranteed to stop you getting the Varsity blues.

© itchy Ltd
Globe Quay
Globe Road
Leeds
LS11 5QG
t: 0113 246 0440 f: 0113 246 0550
e: all@itchymedia.co.uk
www.itchycity.co.uk

ISBN 1-903753-06-6

City Managers: Lisa Ellwood, Simon Gray Editorial Team: John Emmerson, Simon Gray, Ruby Quince, Mike Waugh, Andrew Wood
Design: Matt Wood Cover Design: artscience.net
Maps: Steve Cox at Crumb Eye Design
Contributors: Jessica Gray, Ben Southworth
Acknowledgements: Iain Bailey
Jamie Oliver pictures copyright David Loftus

The views expressed in this publication are those of the authors and contributors and are not necessarily those held by the editors o. publishers. Readers are advised to form their own opinions and we welcome any contributions. All details, listings, addresses, phone numbers are correct to our knowledge at the time of going to print. itchy Ltd cannot be held responsible for any breach of copyright arising from the supply of artwork from advertisers.

THE INDEPENDENT

why not subscribe an

save over 60%

For a limited period only, The Independent would like to offer you the chance to purchase The Independent & Independent on Sunday for only £1.50 a week, with our advanced purchase payment subscription. Payments can be made by simply telephoning

0800 783 1920

quoting REFERENCE ISO1000ITCHY

Offices open Mon to Fri 9am - 9pm, Sat & Sun 10am - 4pm

Answer machine at all other times.

When the application has been processed - which may take up to three weeks - The Independent will send you your fully pre-paid vouchers, which can be redeemed at any news outlet. Alternatively, if you prefer home delivery, please let us know the details of your local participating newsagent (including address and postcode) and we can organise the rest! Your newsagent may charge a nominal fee for this service.

contents

- **6** Restaurants
- **18** Bars
- **22** Pubs
- **34** Clubs
- **40** Cafés
- **44** Gay

- **46** Shopping
- **56** Entertainment
- **66** Body
- **70** Takeaway

- **72** Getting About
- **73** Accommodation
- **74** Index & Map

Jamie Oliver

These itchy guides are fantastic. When it comes to travelling, be it social or business, there's so little time to decide where to go and what to do. I spend half my life darting around all over the place, so when I'm visiting cities that I've never been to before, I like to cut to the chase and get to the right places. The itchy guides are just what I've been looking for.

These guides will definitely help you get the most out of a trip to a new city, and whether it's a two hour visit, a night on the town or a long weekend, the itchy team will push you in the right direction. From where you can find the most cutting-edge R'n'B to the coolest threads, as well as some good grub, a few drinks and maybe have a bit of a boogie. And at long last, someone's cottoned on to the fact that once in a while a dodgy pub and a bit of karaoke, beats posing at the latest bar opening, hands down.

It's reassuring to know that the itchy team take their research seriously. I know from experience that they certainly know how to mix business with pleasure.

– Jamie Oliver

For what's happening right here, right now and in 17 other cities... www.itchycity.co.uk. All the events, all the time, with news on gigs, cinema, restaurants, clubs and more. You can sign up for updates on anything from hip hop to happy hours, vent your anger about our reviews and get discounts for your favourite venues. Whatever's happening in the city, itchycity's there.

And for when you're out, we've made that hulking great big wap-phone actually useful. Next time it's 1am and you're gasping for a Guinness, whip out the wap and find your nearest late bar... **wap.itchycity.co.uk**

itchycity.co.uk

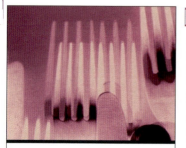

restaurants

www.itchycity.co.uk

American

Chili's
164-167 Abbeygate House, East Road (01223) 505678
God bless America. Cambridge has been graced with Chili's production line style food and US sized portions. Average cow burger selection, with an adjoining cocktail bar, with overeager orders of lurid concoctions flowing across it. You could probably sit here and eat all day if you don't mind putting up with the terrible service, but remember our oversized American friends across the water when asking to go large. You won't look so hot walking across the Grafton Centre with your trouser buttons undone.
Fajitas £10.50 House wine £10.95

Footlights
Grafton Centre (01223) 323434
Looks like the type of place where you'd have to make an effort of Jennifer Lopez proportions, but appearances, thankfully, can be deceptive. Once through the

doors you can let your hair down, slam tequila at the bar or indulge in Latino lustiness with your chosen playmate. There's Italian and Mexican dishes on the menu, so make an impression with your chimichangas and calzone combo.

King prawn fajitas £10.95 HW £8.95

Garfunkel's
21-24 Bridge Street
(01223) 311053/311046

A pyromaniac's playground; the furnishing material of choice being wood, and lots of it. Very friendly and efficient staff, but they don't go in for fancy order requirements, you know, like heated puddings – far too hi-tech. Being situated next door to the eternally busy Café Rouge probably doesn't do them any favours, but hiring a new chef and turning the lights up would be a start.

Spicy platter of steak, Cajun chicken & calamari strips £9.95 HW £9.25

Old Orleans
Millers Yard, 10 Mill Lane
(01223) 322777

When this restaurant first arrived in Cambridge it used to make an effort. The food was warm, service polite and the general vibe relaxing. Now you can expect to be served by monosyllabic monkeys trying their best to mess up your order and wheel you in and out of the place faster than a Mississippi steamboat. If you down a skin full in the adjoining cocktail bar you might appreciate the Deep South experience more, but I wouldn't count on it.

Full rack of ribs £9.95 HW £9.20

English

22 Chesterton Road
22 Chesterton Road (01223) 351880

Deliberately a very exclusive restaurant, thanks in part to its grand launch party, but more because there are only eight tables, so if you ever manage to get a seat you feel that you are among the privileged few. The hype has now somewhat diminished, but it offers some fine traditional English cooking. Its intimacy and picturesque location means couples often seek it out. Well worth booking in advance to secure a table.

Four course set menu £24.50
HW £10.25

Browns
23 Trumpington Street (01223) 461655

Full of all the old favourites, rarely cutting edge but always consistent. You can avoid interminable queues by sitting at the bar, whilst waiting for your number to flash up on the board; a bit like waiting for the cheese counter in Tescos, but with the comfort of a glass of white wine. Always a fashionable choice, but this is just as

much to do with the plush surroundings and the excellent drinks rather than the food.
Steak, mushroom and Guinness pie £7.95 House wine £9.95

No.1 Kings Parade
1 Kings Parade (01223) 359506/354907
Despite paying top dollar for their prime location opposite Kings College, the potential merits of upstairs seating were obviously lost on the proprietors. In its many different guises, successions of managers have tried and failed to really make this place take off. Descend into the restaurant and you'll dine in an old cellar, but even draining several kegs won't make up for the lack of atmosphere. The clientele are equally as dull, and after an obscenely long wait for the food, you're not going to be best impressed with the 15% service charge.
Roast Cod Fillet £10.95 HW £11.00

French

Café Rouge
24-26 Bridge Street (01223) 364961
Very popular among local intellectuals and imitators. If you've not handed in your essay, be aware that you'll probably find your tutor in here banging on about Sartre's theory of self-awareness with the waiter. A French styled chain restaurant, which has remained popular across the country due to its reasonably priced Franglais cuisine. It all smacks of slight pretension, but fortunately there's no pomme frite on its shoulder. The Cambridge version is no different to any other, except that it's a lot darker, but it provides the perfect backdrop for the live jazz played every first Sunday of the month.
Steak baguette £6.95 HW £9.70

The Dome
33-34 St. Andrews Street (01223) 313818
A relatively new Cambridge haunt which has already risen phoenix-like from the ashes of old management. The menu is as strong as ever, and the staff have at last learnt the basics of politeness. If you're just in for a cup of coffee and a flick through the paper, you won't have to worry about impatient waiters trying to wrench you out of your seats. This has worked well as the Dome now has its regulars and considerably more visitors than its namesake in Greenwich ever managed.
Salad Chinoise with chargrilled chicken £6.95 HW £10.95

Hobbs Pavilion
Parker's Piece (01223) 367480
Formerly a cricket pavilion, nestling behind the University Arms Hotel, it's near perfect for relaxing in the summer-

time. No surprises then that it's popular with students who fancy spending some of their loans on something other than cheap cider. If you've got a little nipper then you'll be made particularly welcome. They were awarded a distinction from Egon Ronay for their outstanding children's service. In the winter months it's a whole different ball game, as despite its cosy glow in the darkness, it's difficult to find with poor outside lighting, and the quagmire of mud makes it a challenge to reach, but when you do you'll be rewarded.

Slivers of pan fried lamb with Mediterranean vegetables £9.95
HW £9.95

Michel's Brasserie
21-24 Northampton Street
(01223) 353110

Supposedly haunted, it was the subject of a television documentary a couple of years ago. Apparently you can occasionally see the apparitions of a cloaked figure; enough to put you off your food if it wasn't so good. One to take your partner for a romantic meal, especially if you can get a seat near the open fire. Mind you, it could be more trouble than its worth if you're a fella, some of the waitresses are not easy to take your eyes off.

Red snapper with warm serranno fajita spiced salsa & wilted rocolla £13.95
HW £9.95

TOP FIVE... Eats to impress
1. Midsummer House
2. Loch Fyne
3. Michel's Brasserie
4. Venue
5. Vaults

Midsummer House
Midsummer Common (01223) 369299

It's refreshing that despite being highly revered, Midsummer House is far from pretentious. Situated next to the River Cam, it has an excellent reputation and remains the place to impress people either with some daft statement of social status, or if you simply appreciate fine food. It's no longer that pricey, mainly because its competitors have become more expensive whilst offering considerably less. Make sure you dress up though, as frayed old school blazers might be a statement in some parts of town, but here you'll only disappoint.

Set menu, 3 courses £42 HW £15.95
Pan fried fillet of John Dory, risotto of fresh anchovy, confit of garlic and rosemary beurre blanc

Pierre Victoire
90-92 Regent Street (01223) 570170
Yet another link in a chain of restaurants, so you're probably familiar with what's on offer already. Like slices of Brie, the quality varies, but all the ingredients are the same. Traditional farmhouse décor and wall murals reign supreme. No surprise then that it's popular with those nearing dotage. "Typically French" all you need now's a string of onions around your neck. Chewing on a piece of straw and reeking of garlic is optional, but don't expect to get table priority.
Breast of duck roasted in honey and crushed peppercorns £11.95 HW £7.95

Indian

Cambridge Curry Centre
**45-47 Castle Street
(01223) 363666/302687**
Providing beered-up after-pubbers with proper Indian grub to soak up the booze. The staff are friendly and patient which is useful as some of the clientele struggle to pronounce their own names, let alone their order. If you actually stay sober, you'll notice that the food is actually pretty good – nevertheless the place does tend to be pretty quiet until 11.20pm.
Chicken tikka masala £6.95 HW £6.95

Curry Mahal
Millers Yard, Mill Lane (01223) 360409
Sophistication for all those who don't fancy dribbling curry down their chins. Bright in design and waistcoat, there's no chance of mistaking what's on your plate with all that light. Forget Sunday roast with the old battle-axe, you'd be better off dining from their 'banquet', and they promise they won't say 'You wash, I'll dry' at the end of the meal. Unless of course, you can't pay.
Thalia nawabi £11.95 House wine £8.95

The Gulshan
106 Regent Street (01223) 302330

Classically styled Indian restaurant with the best Indian food in town. My girlfriend likes it creamy, and she was positively frothing at the mouth with the chicken tikka masala. No point beating about the bush, The Gulshan is a cut above, and despite the fact that the waiter was whispering sweet-nothings into my partner's ear, I was more than happy to turn a blind eye and concentrate on the food. How could I compete with culinary skills of this calibre anyway?
Chicken tikka masala £6.95 Pint of Kingfisher £2.60

India House
**31 Newnham Road
(01223) 461661/460173**
Posh venue with neither sight nor sniff of a dodgy curry house. They've even turned their noses up at those compul-

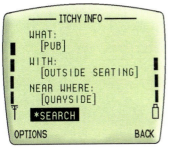

Cheap drinks offers...
direct to your WAP
wap.itchycambridge.co.uk

sory fake flowers and gone for the real thing. Crazy. Mind you, you'd be best advised to lift one from the vase and stick it in your lapel. It really is that smart. Young professionals flock to taste the food without fear of being the butt of many a pissed-up student's jokes. Overlooking the millpond, the location and lack of attitude means it could easily end up over-priced. It's not yet, but give them a chance, they've only just finished polishing the glasses.

Lamb balti £7.95 Pint of Tetley £2.50

The Shalimar
84 Regent Street (01223) 355378

Rudely placed on a street which deserves better, it should've given up the ghost years ago and spared all Cambridge connoisseurs the trauma. Plenty of better alternatives along this road, I suggest you try them instead.

Chicken tikka masala £5.80 Pint of Kingfisher £2.50

Italian

Caffe Uno
32 Bridge Street (01223) 314954

One of the first arrivals in the Quayside area, and still the only restaurant there worthy of note. There are stellar views across The Cam, especially during the summer when you can enjoy a cappuccino outside, and an overall feeling of luxuriant exclusivity, fortunately without a hefty price tag. Appealing to almost everyone from students to your nan. The warmth of the walls is reflected in the service, and you'll have a punt-sized smile once you realise that you've still got change in your pocket at the end of the night.

Linguine di calamari e gamberoni £7.95 HW £9.95

Don Pasquale
12 Market Hill (01223) 367063/350106 (upstairs)

Summer attracts alfresco seated sun worshippers, in all their milk-bottle pale-skinned glory. Southern Italy it'll never be, come on, it's on the corner of Market

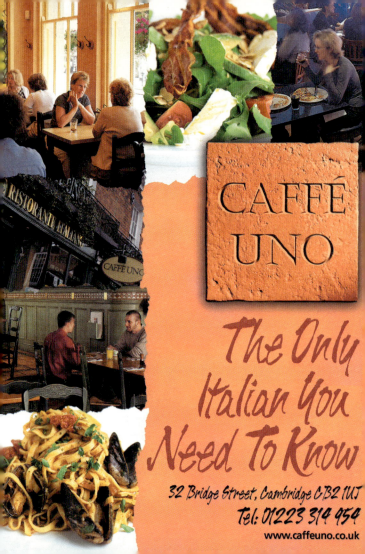

Square, and caters for all and sundry. But they aim to please, doing everything except footing the bill. The downstairs pizzeria's known as 'the one that does Saint Valentino'; one huge pizza created in homage to loved-up couples. If you've come over all exclusive, sit yourself and your over-inflated self-importance in the classy restaurant upstairs.
Saint Valentino £16.50 HW £8.95

La Margherita
15 Magdalene Street (01223) 315232
No cocktails, but a Bible-sized menu and wine list. Put it this way, around fifty dishes means that boredom is unlikely if you like pasta and pizza. Most of the clientele do as they return here with homing pigeon frequency. Still, whilst the food's good, it's not gold plated. So what's the secret? I'd hazard a guess that it's because you'll be as well tended as the owner's window boxes. Check out his petunias.
Smoked salmon fettuccini £8.05
House wine £8.95

La Mimosa
4 Rose Crescent (01223) 362525
Dust off your dancing shoes and wiggle your hips with gyrating gusto, Latino style. What was formerly 'Flambards' (and still referred to as this by many locally), now serves up Italian food, and live music. It holds salsa evenings every Friday night in the basement, and if you're feeling a bit rusty there are lessons beforehand. All this serves to distract from the food, which is of a reasonable standard but not overwhelming, and the waitresses spend more time dancing than attending to the customers. They've managed to stoke up a lively atmosphere so it's more suited to large groups. Those seeking a quiet evening would be advised to seek their thrills elsewhere.
Chicken Pollo Mimosa £11.90 HW £9.90

Pizza Express
7a Jesus Lane (01223) 324033
28 St. Andrews Street (01223) 361320

Same menu, different locations, with the larger of the two housed at Jesus Lane. You can pick a room to suit your mood, but be warned, intellectuals and old buffers opt for the library-style wood panelled option. You're treated to some live jazz and a pianist most evenings, which will help take your mind off the fact that you've finished your meal and you're still starving. Once you've finished you can pop downstairs to Po Na Na, and see if they've got any peanuts to chew on.
Pizza Florentina £6.40 HW £10.95

Trattoria Pasta Fresca
66 Mill Road (01223) 352836
Winner of the PAPA National Pasta Restaurant of the Year Award 1999. Which I'm sure means a lot more to them than it does me, and says a lot more about the place than I can tell you. Very simple in design, but you're going for the freshly prepared food rather than the chance to spot any statues.
Cannelloni Rossini £8.95
House wine £11.45 per litre

Oriental

Charlie Chan
14 Regent Street
(01223) 361763/359336
I don't know Charlie Chan, but you've got to hand it to the guy, he's sussed out that gullible English people will happily pay more to eat upstairs than downstairs in his restaurant. With the usual restaurant stuff downstairs, upstairs it metamorphoses into the 'Blue Lagoon', where everything is exactly the same but with some very average live music. If you're a platinum card poser, then this might seem like a good way to show off, but with overpriced and indifferent food you'll only look a bit of a Charlie (sorry).
1/4 Crispy duck £8.80 HW £10.50

Chato
2-4 Lensfield Road
(01223) 363129/364115
Quality Singaporian restaurant for those of you looking for an alternative take on your noodles. Plenty of set menus to choose from, including a vegetarian option if you're too lazy to make your own decisions, but it's best to be adventurous. The aubergine dish is a real beauty, as long as you like aubergines. Not cheap, but then neither am I, well, not all the time.
Chicken satay £4.50 HW £9.50

Chopsticks
22a Magdalene Street (01223) 566510

It doesn't look good on first view. Cracked windows, microscopically small and very smoky. Get down to what you're there for though, the food, and you can't go wrong. Due to its size and popularity you'd be wise to book ahead, and you can bring your own bottle without a corkage fee. Anything you can't polish off there and then can be scooped up into a doggy bag and taken home for breakfast.
Special Szechuan noodles £6.00
No corkage charge

Peking Restaurant
21 Burleigh Street (01223) 354755
Dodgy 60s décor runs amok in a place that's practically an institution, it's been

Names and occupations?
Claire and Kim, nanny and financial wizard
Where can I buy you a drink?
Champagne please...All Bar One, Quinns
Where do you become Dancing Queens? Fez Club, The Junction
Intimate meal for 3? Browns, Gulshan
What excites you? Punting, holding hands by the river with my man
Ooh exciting, what turns you off?
Bloody cyclists, lack of parking

here so long. The food's all prepared by the delicate hand of the proprietor, apparently, so he must have mixed feelings when he gets a party of twenty in for the night. He's good at his job mind you, although he has a natural aversion to credit cards. They're not accepted here so make sure you visit the hole in the wall before-hand.

Mixed seafood noodles £14 HW £11

Thai

Sala Thong
35 Newnham Road (01223) 323178
Have your elbows at the ready as it's so small you'll have to barge your way to your seat. Stacked full of students, not surprisingly, because it's pretty cheap, and word of cheap red curry no doubt travels back to the colleges pretty quickly. The set menus change every week, but sadly not a thong in sight.
**Green chicken curry £6.50
HW £9.25 per litre**

Thai Regent
108 Regent Street (01223) 464355
Genuine Thai food with a wide selection of vegetarian dishes. I'm no connoisseur of Thai cooking, but this is pretty run-of-the-mill fare. Judging by the amount of empty tables most people would tend to agree with me.
Cow Pad Na Kai £7.75 HW £9.75

Vegetarian

Rainbow
9a Kings Parade (01223) 321551
OK, so you won't find gold at the end of the corridor, and there's not a kid's TV programme in sight, but they do have imagination, which is great news for carnivores and carrot nibblers alike. Blink and you'll miss it, this is a hideaway for those in the know, with a menu inspired by traditional, round-the-world dishes, minus the dead flesh elements. A small place with big offerings, it's just about the food; the only real downside is the lack of Zippy and Bungle.
**Spinach lasagne £6.25 Organic
HW £10.95**

 Cheap meal offers sent to your phone
wap.itchycambridge.co.uk

Other/Fusion

Dojo Noodle Bar
1-2 Millers Yard, Mill Lane
(01223) 363471

Their aim is to provide a wide range of Pacific Rim dishes at minimal expense. That's what they tell you, and the lads done well, achieving all their goals. Your food comes in huge bowls, and is served faster than a Samurai warriors slice. Hugely popular and hugely impressive, the superest noodles in town.
Gyu Yaki-Soba £4.95 House wine £8.50

Efes
78 King Street (01223) 500005
Don't expect to simply book a table, they only do slots, so be sure your date is a control freak about time keeping as they'll give you one hour only and then your times up. It leaves a bad taste in the mouth, a bit like most kebabs, that they're in such a hurry to get rid of you. Shame really as the food's very good, but if you're gonna push me around I ain't coming back.
Set menu £14.95 HW £9.80 per carafe

The Galleria
33 Bridge Street (01223) 362054
With a picture-perfect view, you would have thought that the chef would be inspired by the location, but the menu here is far from creative. Opt for a snack in the summertime, when the terrace tempts tourists and locals alike into drinking copious amounts of wine. No one really goes for the food anyway, more for the ambience, which is a good job too as you'd be rather disappointed if you'd set yourself up for a decent meal.
Salmon crackling with red pepper sauce £10.50 HW £9.50

Loch Fyne
Trumpington Street (01223) 362433
Scottish cooking at its best, particularly the seafood, which is some of the best this side of the border. Despite being open for some time now, it has remained one of those places which people tell their friends about in hushed and reverential tones – presumably in the hope that no-one will overhear and leave them without a table. It shouldn't be a problem as there's plenty of seating, but grub this good is unlikely to go unnoticed. If food's an art form, then the cuisine served here should be displayed in the Fitzwilliam Museum across the road. A firm itchy favourite.
Bradan Orach £8.95 HW £9.95

Vaults
14a Trinity Street (01223) 506090
Recently refurbished and extended to the tune of one million pounds. I'd like to say it was money well spent, but I can't. It takes more than a zinc bar to warrant that sort of expenditure. Regardless of that the food is still of a particularly high quality, especially the seafood. Probably the best time to visit is on a Sunday lunchtime. You can listen to some live blues, and tuck into a very tasty roast lunch. Alternatively you can have a go on the internet terminals and log onto www.itchycambridge.co.uk to see all that's going on in the city.
Chargrilled swordfish with dill mayonnaise and parsnip crisps £6.50 HW £9.50

Venue
66 Regent Street (01223) 367333
Live weekend music and cartoons dotting the walls, the entire place is designer-trendy. White walls, light wooden tables, with a splattering of pink, red and orange, not forgetting the black piano. The people at Venue are fanatical about fresh food, even the bread's cooked on the premises, and if you're looking for

cooking with a twist, then this is the venue for you. They're very proud of their concoctions as well, so don't expect your food in a flash. It's not a problem though, you can pop upstairs for a cocktail or two while you wait. Splendid.
Pan seared fillets of sea bass with warm roasted vegetable salad, salsa verde and sauce vierge £15.25 HW £10.95

Yippee
7-9 King Street (01223) 518111

A new arrival on the Cambridge restaurant scene. It looks like something straight out of a Habitat catalogue with the blonde wood tables and Mark Rothko prints. Clean air accompanies the minimalism, so smokers will have to grab a quick ciggie outside. It all looks as though they've studied Dojo and decided to have a go themselves. Nothing wrong with that as there's plenty of room for two noodle bars in town, except this one isn't nearly as appetising as the other. I don't know if they'd over-ordered on the week's supply of beansprouts when I went, but there was enough in my bowl to keep Jack happy. Yippee indeed.
Tom Yum Udon £8.25 Glass of saki £3.20

bars

www.itchycity.co.uk

All Bar One

**36-37 St. Andrews Street
(01223) 371081**

Lunching lawyers abound, so if you're after some free legal advice, pull up a pew. After dark it's surprisingly lively for somewhere in which you can usually always grab a table. You'll know the format by now – school dining hall appearance, big clock, newspapers etc. – but it would take an effort of Keith Floyd dimensions to get through their mammoth wine list. Difficult to criticise, and equally difficult to rave about, although it's still the only place in town where you'll find grown men reading The Beano – and yes, that is a good thing.

Bar 8

Guildhall Place (01223) 477900

Previously home to the Job Centre, now Cambridge's latest addition to a less than substantial bar scene. Still attracting job dodgers, except these ones are just waiting to burn a hole in their student loans. If you've got the time, money and stomach for it you can spend the whole day in here. The doors open at 10am

Name and occupation?
Steven The Ba, Merchant banker
Ryhming slang? Where do you spend your millions? Quinns
Puh, bankers. Where do you shake your moneymaker? Po Na Na
What about power-lunching?
The Gulshan
You clearly don't dress to impress, but where can we find such garms?
Cult Clothing. I'm going, time is money.

and a late licence keeps the drinks flowing 'til 2am everyday except the Sabbath. Should you manage the feat, you'll see a whole host of folk throughout the day. The daytime shoppers grab the best seats by the windows taking their time over tea and coffee, whilst the office crowd make the most of the excellent menu on offer. By night the students move in, and the noise levels move up a few decibels. Far more rewarding than applying for vacant bricklaying jobs.

Bar Moosh
1-3 Station Road (01223) 360268
Rarely a soul in sight during the day, bar a few lunchtime diners, but once the trains start spilling out the rat race crew things start to liven up – but not much. If you're not suitably attired then you can expect a few sneering glances from the locals who appear far too familiar with each other. Ignore the office geeks by commandeering the battered sofa, and down a bottle of wine by candlelight. Or plonk yourself down in the dining-area and take advantage of the very reasonably priced food menu. The live jazz on Thursdays provides plenty of entertainment, not so much for the music, but for the chin-stroking appreciation society. Cambridge pretension at its very worst.

Browns
23 Trumpington Street (01223) 461655
Mercs and Porsches used to line the street outside, and the atmosphere was decidedly stuffy inside. Now it's relaxed its upper lip, the place is a far more enjoyable experience. There's still the traditional older folk, looking slightly bemused by the transformation, but at

least you can shield yourself away in the bar area if you're only in for a drink. Splendid cocktail selection served by people who at least look as if they know what they're doing.

CC's Sports Bar

Sturton Street (01223) 716309

Homage to all things athletic, you can even hire out the old-style gymnasium out the back, if staring at a screen and lifting a pint to your lips seems too exertion-free. Eight big screens beam out the best sporting action, and if you're camera shy it's best to avoid upstairs as the Red TV crew regularly film here. Ideal for large groups to hire out the sectioned off dining area, especially as you can pick your choice of music and lighting. Fortunately they don't tend to attract Marilyn Manson fans.

Ha Ha @ The Blue Boar

17 Trinity Street (01223) 305089

It used to be the Blue Boar, and out of respect, it even makes reference to the fact. But some of us can't forget that the Blue Boar was simply the best drinking establishment in town, and change has definitely not been for the better in this instance. Still, at the end of the day, you can always put down some new floorboards and finish it off with little aluminium touches, but that never replaces the stuff that Cambridge legends are made of. It's yet to get as busy as The Blue Boar did on a quiet night, but then some of the best places do start off slowly.

Henry's

Quayside (01223) 324649

Students, young professionals and the odd tourist rub shoulders, elbows and any other bodily part necessary, in the crush to get to the bar. That's in the evenings when most people have had a few. Come along during the day or sit down for a meal at the back and it's all rather polite. Probably due to the clientele leaning the wrong side of forty. I doubt they come here for the cuisine, rather the fact it has excellent views over

the River Cam. Extremely busy at the weekends, which I can only put down to Cambridge's lack of bars, because Henry's is looking decidedly past its sell by date these days.

Quay Bar
Quayside (01223) 556961

If the imaginative name's anything to go by, this place is going to be a roaring success. Maybe it's a clue as to the 'grey matter' potential of the crowd they're aiming to attract. If they still can't figure out where it is, someone put them out of their misery and book them a 'room' at Fulbourn. It's too early to tell what types will frequent this 'style-bar' but I'd hazard a guess at the old Bar Coast crew, oh, and a few kleptomaniac magpies, drawn in by the sparkling silver interior.

Rat and Parrot
Downing Street (01223) 304357
Thompsons Lane (01223) 311701

If you've ever been within smelling distance of one Rat, you'll know what to expect. The Thompsons Lane venue at least has the advantage of looking out

onto the river and Jesus Green, and being slightly off the beaten track, the crowd are a touch more reserved than their counterparts in Downing St. Unless you're on the pull, then the other Rat is best given a wide berth. Two floors of Ben Sherman shirt and loafer combos are two floors too many. Townie infested, all looking remarkably similar, and probably all called Kev. Best viewed through your beer goggles if you're going to make the most of it. But then, if that's the case, it won't really matter where you are will it?

Venue
66 Regent Street (01223) 367333

Above the restaurant you'll find a cocktail bar, that's if you can get past the committed bouncers who won't just let any old riff-raff through the doors. The surroundings are far more laid back, and you can indulge yourself on probably the finest cocktail menu in town. Don't let the names put you off either; 'Rigour Mortis' and 'Brain Haemorrhage' will leave you with nothing more than a sweet smile on your face. At least until the morning.

pubs

www.itchycity.co.uk

Opening hours Mon-Sat 11am-11pm, Sun 12pm-10.30pm, unless stated.

The Alma
26 Russell Court (01223) 364965

Saturated by sixth-formers with a dribbling of dodgy old men trying to pull them thrown in for good measure, dragging the average age up to something approaching decent. Pool maestros pitch up against one another, as the girls bending over the table to line up their shot cause much groin-twitching amongst garrulous oldies who should know better. Food: 12pm-3pm

The Anchor
Silver Street (01223) 353554

Popular hangout for students, comically filled with James Bond look-a-likes in dapper slacks. You'd think it'd be Martini territory but there's some serious pint swilling going on across the Anchor's three floors. Given its name, it's impressively awash with alcohol, and come summer it's popular with punters in their punts effeminately knocking back tumblers of Pimms. Bag an outside seat by the river and hope for some ram-raiding. It's not big and it's not clever, but it is amusing.

Baron of Beef

19 Bridge Street (01223) 505022

Simple, sparse pub with an extremely long bar. You get 'em all in here – hardcore drinkers scratching at the doors come 11am, students relaxing after a strenuous lecture, and daytime shoppers enjoying a stiff one after hammering the credit cards. I can think of no good reason, besides working there, why you'd want to spend a whole night in the Beef, but it's well worth a quick one on the way into town on a night out.
Food: Mon-Thurs 12pm-3pm, 5pm-8pm, Sat 12pm-5.30pm, Sun 12pm-4pm

Bath House

3 Bene't Street (01223) 350969

Timbered 13th century building heaving with history, and some of the locals look like they were there supping mead when it first threw open its doors. Nothing's sacred though, so this is now owned by the Hogshead, who have typically placed some unsuitably colourful chairs inside. That said, it's still a relaxing venue in which to sink a few daytime ales with friends or a paper, if you can put up with the constant drone of American accents that is.
Food: Sun-Thurs 12pm-9pm, Fri/Sat 12pm-8pm

The Boat House

14 Chesterton Road (01223) 460905

Beer and blokes – there's a surprise, but here it's all guest ales, tight-gusseted men and a sprinkling of in-the-know women. But before you get carried away thinking that Cambridge has finally thrown stereotypes to the wind, you should probably know that in fine tradition, the guys are actually rowers. You'll find this lot waxing their chests, but you won't catch them prancing around in a pink feather boa and heels. Well, not in public anyway. Feel free to try and dip your cox in the water.
Open: Mon-Sat 12pm-11pm
Food: Fri-Mon 12pm-4pm, Tues-Thurs 12pm-7pm

The Bun Shop

1 King Street (01223) 366866

From the outside this place bears an uncanny resemblance to one of those nasty council estate pubs you find littered around Essex. Never judge a book by its cover I was always told, and that's certainly true of the Bun Shop. There's a multitude of choices once you step inside. You can check out the restaurant, wine and tapas bars or just snuggle up inside the saloon bar. You'll no doubt come across 'The Oak Joke (deceased)' pun, which isn't funny – it's just a suspended punt that's clearly seen better days. Read the explanation, and laugh as

heartily as if it had just fallen down and smacked you on the head or stare vacantly wondering what the hell it's got to do with buns.
Closed Sundays
Tapas available every evening

Burleigh Arms
9 Newmarket Road (01223) 301547
If you're into throwing yourself in at the deep end of tradition, don't come here. Despite the efforts to make it appear a quaint ancient tavern, the place is newer than Britney Spears' chest, and about as genuine too. Not that this really matters to the hordes of twenty-somethings who tirelessly return here. Mind you, it's not what it looks like, it's what's on offer that counts. Beer will always be beer at the end of the day, and some people will never care about where they drink it.
Open: 11.30pm-3pm, 5.30pm-11pm
Food: 12pm-3pm, 6pm-9pm

The Cambridge Blue
85-87 Gwydir Street (01223) 361382
The Twilight Zone revisited, what with the unsurprisingly imaginative blue exterior, and the silence of an entertainment-free zone. With no music, fruit machines, or TV to take refuge in, there's more pressure to actually try and talk to your mates or partner. If you get stuck you could always turn to the memorabilia that lines the walls, but after that you're on your own. Guaranteed to sort out the 'speak to their partner' men from the 'stare at the screen' boys.
Open: 12pm-2.45pm, 5.30pm-11pm
Food: 12pm-2pm, 6pm-11pm

The Castle
37 St. Andrews Street (01223) 506200
Nestling between All Bar One and Wetherspoon's and probably none too sure if that's for the best. On the plus side they get a lot of passing trade from the influx of new bars in the area, but the downside is that most of them are only interested in supping a tonic water. Still the hardcore regulars remain, and no amount of Prada handbags will force them to find refuge elsewhere.
Food: Mon-Sat 12pm-7pm

Castle Inn
38 Castle Street (01223) 353194
If sampling specialist ales is your bag, then there's nine Adnams beers on tap to savour inside or on the patio. Plus, there's a 'no teams allowed' policy, which spares you the sight of rugger-buggers with their shorts around thier ankles, displaying their usually less than impressive tackles. Some of the best pub grub in town.
Open: Mon-Fri 11.30am-3pm, 3.30pm-11pm, Sat/Sun 11.30am-3pm, 6pm/7pm-11/10.30pm
Food: 11.45am-2.15pm, 6pm-9.15pm

Champion of the Thames
68 King Street (01223) 352043

Does anyone give a shit about the Boat Race anymore? Obviously those involved do, and their friends and family, but come on, do you know who won the last one? Fortunately no one inside this tiny pub cares either. It's the kind of place where the walls are plastered with pictures of locals in various inebriated poses. You might feel as though you're intruding on someone's private party when you walk in, but don't worry – they don't mind as long as you don't get in the way of their drinking and wild stories. Grab a table by the open fire and talk about inconsequential matters – like the Boat Race. And as unbelievable as it sounds, the Thames now has Tuesday night live music sessions. It was one of those 'best kept secrets', but the cat's well and truly out of the bag now. A true itchy favourite.

Coach and Horses
Trumpington High Street, Trumpington (01223) 506248
Although not in the centre of Cambridge, it's definitely worth a Sunday lunchtime visit, especially if you're looking for a touch of civilisation after the weekend's excesses. You could wheel the old man out for a swifty, or your extended family for a sit-down meal. In truth, it's a suburban ale-house, and in this area they're as common as a two pence piece, but that hasn't stopped it from being the fave of the Trumpington locals, particularly at weekends when it's packed to the wooden beams.
Open: Mon-Fri 12pm-3pm, 5.30pm-11pm, Sat/Sun 12pm-3pm, 6pm-11pm/10.30pm
Food: 12pm-2.30pm, 6.30-9.15pm

The Cricketers
18 Melbourne Place (01223) 508255
They're more into red balls than Red Bull here. With that in mind, strap on your pads, adjust your box and march in with the confidence of Brian Lara. It's a nice pub, but the regulars are annoyingly dreary, and fire hostile glances at you like a

bouncer from Curtley Ambrose. Do you know how many test runs Geoffrey Boycott scored? If you give a toss, then this is the place for you, if not give it a body swerve.

Open: 12pm-11pm
Food: 12pm-2.30pm, 6pm-9pm

Devonshire Arms
1 Devonshire Road (01223) 316610

If you're into reggae and dub, come here on Monday nights and indulge. On top of that, it's got a late licence, which in Cambridge is about as rare as a state-educated student. Plus, there's a family run atmosphere and everyone's welcome. Bring your granny and dance to music influenced by outlawed horticulture. From Elvis to Alvin, come and rock. Late licence 'til 12am Fri, Sat and whenever else they can be arsed.

The Eagle
8 Bene't Street (01223) 505020

One of Cambridge's finer drinking establishments. Plenty of rooms, including a

no-smoking area to fence the boring ones off, an outside courtyard, and roaring open fires to warm your cockles in the winter. Make sure you check out the back room – the ceiling's covered in RAF, American Air Force and World War II pilots' signatures, just don't get in the way of anal, snap-happy tourists, clicking away with paparazzi fervour. The kind of place that's just begging to be host to an all-day session.

Food: 12pm-2.30pm, 5pm-late

The Empress
72 Thoday Street (01223) 247236

Impressively supplying the local student community with yet another excuse to skive, and allowing long-standing regulars to see what their taxes get spent on. It's named after the old Queen Vic but you won't catch Peggy Mitchell tending bar or her two 'lovely boys' hanging about and looking for 'outside naaw' trouble. Probably why it's so popular. Just off Mill Road, it's worth making an effort to find, but remember, if you reach Arthur's allotments you've gone too far.

TOP FIVE...
Places to pull
1. **The Regal**
2. **Fifth Avenue**
3. **Rat & Parrot**
4. **Ha Ha's**
5. **The Locomotive**

Fort St. George
Midsummer Common (01223) 354327
This is one of those isolated, made for summer pubs that Cambridge seems to do so well, playing a never-ending stream of 80s classics, and with an outside area, where you can sit gazing pseudo-reflectively at the river or salute the flag of St. George that flies proudly. Look at your wallet though and you'll realise you've been relieved of a small fortune, just for a couple of pints. Come winter, it suddenly seems to be on the other side of the world, detached and bleak, and falling flat on its sunburnt face. It should be nicknamed "the dragon" because it fought St. George (ho ho). But it isn't.
Open: Mon-Thurs 11am-3pm, 5pm-11pm, Fri-Sun 11am-11pm
Food: Mon-Fri 11am-3pm, 6pm-9pm, Sat/Sun 11am-9pm

The Fountain Inn
12 Regent Street (01223) 366540
To all intents and purposes a pub for the more mature drinker; it's referred to amongst twenty-somethings as 'that old man's pub'. The building's impressive, but

on this stretch of road, sheer pub numbers dictate that it needs more than an impressive exterior to get a top rating. If you're into people spotting, prepare to be disappointed by the unassuming office workers there for a quiet pint and a scan of the paper, but if that's your nirvana then you'll slip amongst the suits nicely.

Free Press
Prospect Row (01223) 368337
Although smaller than a gnat's g-string, this is one of Cambridge's finest, but it's non-smoking, which is surely alienating most of your potential custom. With a reasonably-priced range of ales and standard brews (all served with impeccable grace), it's often filled with bearded, open-toed sandal-wearing folk, discussing medieval battering rams. Unsurprisingly, the clean air proves to be many an eco-warrior's sanctuary – after no tabs and eight pints of Broadside it's very tempting to show them what a proper battering is all about.
Open: 12pm-2.30pm, 6pm-11pm
Food: 12pm-2pm

The Globe
21 Hills Road (01223) 353997
Bog standard boozer, serving typical food and ale at bargain basement prices. Best for when you're only after simple food, or meeting an illicit lover – you'll save a penny or two and are unlikely to bump into friends. Unless they're doing the same thing. Make sure you pick somewhere slightly more interesting to trade the stories though.
Food: 12pm-2pm, 6pm-9pm

The Graduate
16 Chesterton Road (01223) 324325

Formerly a Firkin pub until they firked off, and let that equally tedious 'it's a scream' lot take over and paint the thing a garish shade of yellow. Giant Jenga and Connect 4 keep the potential nuclear scientists happy as they dent their bank accounts making use of their yellow cards. I suppose an afternoon in here beats any seminar, but you wouldn't want to make a habit of it. There aren't any Hoffman look-a-likes, but there are plenty of students with glazed expressions – presumably dreaming of seducing one another's mothers.

The Granta
14 Newnham Road (01223) 505016
Overlooking the millpond, with punts for hire alongside, it's picture postcard perfect, but where in Cambridge isn't? What really matters though is what's on offer inside, and here it's standard stuff all the way, with the pre-requisite beer and jukebox crowd pleasers. If it's not warm enough to sit outside then don't bother.
Closed Sunday
Food: 12pm-3pm, 6pm-9pm

Green Man
59 High Street, Grantchester (01223) 841178
Cheapskate-priced alehouse and eatery, with food veering from phenomenal to fake. Like all Beefeaters, big groups and birthday bashes litter the place, which begs the question what sort of person hosts a party in a place like this? Take a good look round and you'll find out. The low beamed bar usually catches out a few newcomers, but it's a bad sign when your entertainment comes from watching people crown themselves.
Open: Mon-Fri 11am-2.30pm, 5.30pm-11pm. All day w/e
Food: Mon-Thurs 12pm-2pm, 7pm-9pm, Fri 12pm-2pm, 7pm-9.30pm, Sat 12pm-3pm, 6.30pm-9.30pm, Sun 12pm-6pm

Hogshead
69-73 Regent Street (01223) 323405
Backing onto Parker's Piece, it's desirable to workers, weekenders, youngsters and oldies alike. OK, so everyone's welcome, and everyone seems to make an appearance, especially at weekends. If there's going to be any student bashing, then it's going to be here. Be warned though, the next time you feel like venting some anger the bouncers will have you face down in the grass left to ponder whether the local pooper-scooper population are ever going to be as vigilant as they claim.
Food: Mon-Thurs 12pm-9pm, Fri-Sat 12pm-8pm

King Street Run
86 King Street (01223) 328900
The people let loose with a paintbrush in

this place have clearly been taking some very bad (or good – depends on your perspective) drugs. It's a bit of a mess to be frank, apart from the table football room, which has a cool football crowd mural. The regulars are a diverse lot, most are pleasant enough, but you do get the odd pisshead stumbling in from Christ's Piece breathing stale alcohol over you trying to cadge a fag or money or both. One of the few alternative pubs in town with a clear identity of its own, sing along merrily to the likes of the Manics and the positively joyful Smiths blasting from the jukebox.

Live and Let Live

40 Mawson Road (01223) 460261

Live and let live, my arse. The reception you get when you walk in here is only slightly less chilly than skinny dipping in the River Cam in January. Expect a silence to descend upon entering if your face is unfamiliar, apart from the Irish musicians who only stop to take a sip of their Guinness. A thousand eyes will follow you to the bar or am I just paranoid? Does my bum look big in this?

Open: daily 11.30am-2.30pm, 5.30pm-11pm, Sun 'til 10.30pm
Food: 12pm-2pm, 6pm-9pm (excl. Sun evenings)

The Locomotive

44 Mill Road (01223) 322190

Madder than a Hatter's tea party with almost as much space as Wonderland. Plenty of students on the pull, but if you can't compete with such smooth movers, there's a back room where you can sit and pretend you weren't interested anyway. Pool tables, live music and a

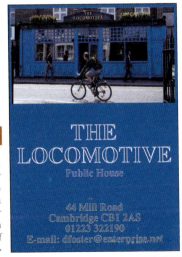

THE INDEPENDENT The best writers, the sharpest opinions

handful of dodgy dancers falling about the place thrown in for good measure. A firm itchy favourite, and not just because their regular band shares the same name. Easily pleased. Us? Never.

The Maypole

Park Street (01223) 352999

Plenty of space inside to mill about, but no maypole to twirl around. Take your pick from the two bars downstairs, the upstairs area easily missed by the casual visitor or the small outside seating area with a cracking view of the multi-storey car park. It's rarely busy on the occasions I've been in and it looks like my grandmother's sitting room (apart from the fifty-inch TV, and a smaller bottle of gin). Food: 11.30am-2.30pm, 5pm-9pm

The Mill

14 Mill Lane (01223) 357026

If ever a pub was made for the summer then it's The Mill. It's as close as Cambridge gets to Ibiza as half the town seems to pile down here. It might as well go into hibernation during the winter. Once the sun comes out it's a big free for all at the bar to get your booze served in shitty plastic cups, but it's all worth it in the end as you bag a space on Sheep's Green. Keep a keen eye out for the cow pats though, many a pair of chinos have been ruined in spectacular fashion. I once spotted a couple going for it hammer and tongs, he ruined his chinos as well, but with stains of a different kind.

The Mitre

17 Bridge Street (01223) 358403

Situated next to the Baron of Beef, and another popular haunt with the tourist crowd who are suckers for a real open fire. It's a very nice fire, but it can't disguise the fact that The Mitre resembles Steptoe's front room. Plenty of guest beers for the real ale aficionados, and also plenty of stupid pearls of wisdom splattered across the walls. Dull, expensive and lacking in any sort of atmosphere. And that's just its good points. Food: 12pm-2.30pm

The Pickerel Inn

30 Magdalene Street (01223) 355068

At 600 years old this place lays claim to being the oldest pub in Cambridge. Once a coaching inn, a brothel and now home to the town and gown brigade. The red light may have gone, but there's still some rather dubious behaviour taking place when one of the many drinking societies are in for the night. It's still kept its olde worlde look, bar the fruit machines, so watch out for all those low cut beams. Food: 11am-8pm

Quinn's

Crowne Plaza Hotel, Downing Street (01223) 464466

Irish theme pubs, lets face it, are usually

crap. Anyone who's ever been to Dublin will appreciate that you can't beat the real deal, but Quinn's is the closest I've seen to bridging the gap. I'm a Guinness fanatic, and so are these chaps with the numerous signs of worship dotted around, so I suppose I was always going to like it here. It comes into its own though with the clientele. By day you can relax upstairs with the complimentary papers in relative isolation, but by night the place becomes one of the most buzzing pubs in town. The dickheads will cram into the Rat & Parrot across the road, but the in-the-know Cambridge folk choose Quinn's. Also the best place in town to watch live sport, especially the rugby. Like I said it's not quite the genuine article, but they give it a good craic (what a rascal – ed)

Food: 11am-7pm

The Regal

St. Andrews Street (01223) 366459

Housed in the former Odeon cinema, a building in which I was introduced to the finer aspects of life courtesy of the back row. Nowadays it's owned by

Wetherspoon's, and lays claim to being the biggest pub in Britain (how many of those have you come across?). Sadly the only aspect of excitement revolves around angry OAPs complaining about the size of the head on their beer. Uncannily, it still resembles the foyer of the cinema with a disarming lack of seating and atmosphere. The townies don't seem to mind as they fill the place every weekend, but some people will go anywhere to save a few pence on the price of a pint.

Food: Mon-Sat 11am-10pm, Sun 12pm-9pm

The Rock

200 Cherry Hinton Road (01223) 505005

Quite a trek from the city centre, but for sports fans this is the place to go. The Rock comes alive and awash with alcohol when there's a big match on the large screens. The locals don't seem to mind who's playing as long as it gives them a chance to let off some steam. There's a definite favouritism towards West Ham,

Name and occupation?
Mark, Decorator

Where do you paint the town red?
Rat & Parrot and Kambar

What about if you forget your packed lunch? Curry Mahal

Best thing about the city apart from the wallpaper? Summer drinking

What makes you want to paint elsewhere? Too many foreign students

so Cambridge's small army of Man United fans have to keep their boasting in check. You can also catch some live music courtesy of various local bands at the weekends. Abandon all hope of having a quiet pint in here.
Food: Mon-Fri 6pm-8.45pm

Rupert Brooke
2 Broadway, Grantchester (01223) 840295
Named after the poet who resided in Grantchester, so you can expect a handful of English Lit students popping in to see where he once stood. It's hard to imagine that old Rupe managed to draw so much inspiration from this place, and it's perfectly feasible to imagine that some of the locals are still propping up the bar as they were in Brooky's day. For the cause of authenticity the management have decided that re-decorating is a no-no, and it shows. Some things never change either, as the great one pointed out, "Cambridge people rarely smile". Not when they spend too much time in this place they don't.

The Salisbury Arms
76 Tenison Road (01223) 576363
Probably the best, certainly the busiest, pub in the Mill Road area. If you make more than the odd appearance you'll become familiar with the dedicated hardcore of regulars. The students in the surrounding area are suitably catered for with a choice of over 35 real ales and a wide and varied food menu, including a whole host of vegetarian dishes. Add on to this the general laid-back atmosphere, the welcoming bar staff and the excellent jukebox and you've got one of Cambridge's essential watering holes. Still not sure what to make of that very scary man suspended from the ceiling riding his bicycle though.
Open: Mon-Thurs 12pm-2.30pm, 6pm-11pm, Sat 12pm-11pm
Food: Served 'til 8pm (exc. Tues, Sat, Sun)

Spread Eagle
67 Lensfield Road (01223) 566291
A traditional pub that rewards loyalty. The Spread's discount offer will cost you a couple of quid, giving you 10% off all food and drinks, and entry into the raffle nights – first prize a bottle of gin (now you're talking). Lazy lunchers can fax food orders through, so your meal's sitting waiting, even if your date's not.
Food: 12pm-2.30pm, 5.30pm-8pm

Square and Compasses
46 High Street, Gt. Shelford
(01223) 843273
Civilised country pub, which has made something of a name for itself in the area. Small, but full of character, and still stubbornly refusing to accept the arrival of the 21st Century. Music, mobile phones and any form of boisterousness are outlawed, but if you fancy a game of arrows then this is the place — that's if you can get near the oche.
Food: 12pm-2pm, 6.30pm-8pm

St. Radegund
127 King Street (01223) 311794

Classic C.A.M.R.A. pub, and the smallest pub in town, apparently. Slightly eccentric place full of customs such as paying for a friend's drink, and if they haven't arrived they'll stick a note on the beam, for them to collect at their leisure. And I still haven't fathomed out what all the graffiti scrawled across the ceiling means. You can sometimes catch live jazz, and indulge in some of their legendary Polish vodkas. Friday nights are given over to the Vera Lynn gin-drinking club. Not sure what it's got to do with every serviceman's favourite lady, but you can be sure that they'll meet again.

The Tram Depot
5 Dover Street (01223) 324553
Former depot of the Cambridge Tramway complete with the original tram rails outside. Fortunately, you're not likely to find any anoraked transport-spotters inside, as this has become a firm favourite with the student crowd. Attitude free with a tasty menu and numerous guest beers to pore over. In keeping with tradition, the Depot is usually the start of the journey before moving on into town, although once settled you may decide that this is the end of the line.
Food: Mon-Sat 12pm-9pm, Sun 12pm-3pm

The Wrestlers
337 Newmarket Road (01223) 566553
Looks like a working man's pub, and you'd half expect it to be full of miners. But since it serves the best Thai food this side of Bangkok, it's full of impoverished students and young couples, who aren't put off by the distressing green walls, but choose instead to gaze in awe at their plates. Just a word of caution, Guinness and Thai food don't sit comfortably, no matter how much you wish they did.
Open: Mon-Sat 12pm-3pm, 5pm-11pm, Closed Sun
Food: 12pm-3pm, 5pm-9pm

clubs

www.itchycity.co.uk

Fez Club
15 Market Passage (01223) 519224

Combining a Turkish and Egyptian ambiance with a smattering of any other North African country you'd care to think of. All that really matters though, is that it's busy every night of the week, catering to Cambridge's classier crowd. Students mingle freely with working types beneath fabric-draped ceilings, schmoozing and flirting throughout the cavernous interior. Predominantly it puts on great house and garage nights, and if that's your bag then dance around it. Or at least keep to the sides attempting to look cool. The whole place lets its hair down on Mondays and Tuesdays with a selection of classic cheese from the last three decades. No fake cool here, just plenty of Cambridge's young and beautiful up for a good night.

Fifth Avenue
Heidelberg Gardens, Lion Yard (01223) 364222

With its roots firmly laid in tack (it used to be called Cinderella's), the last few years have seen Fifth branching out. House and garage are pumped out at the weekends, obviously in an attempt to attract a slightly more discerning crowd. They should

stick to what they do best – mainstream music for mainstream people. When they keep to the tried and trusted methods you can usually have quite a funny night. Hang around for the last dance and catch the men circling the dance floor like vultures only to pull the same bird time and again, because no one else is interested. It's all rather predictable, but at least you know what to expect. As with many clubs like this, you can only really cope with their cheesy choons and meathead punters after a vat of ale, and the reasonably cheap beer is presumably a kind gesture from the management. Added to this, the bouncers will take great delight in refusing entry for inappropriate footwear – which is probably the best thing that could happen to you.

The Junction
Clifton Road (01223) 511511
Besides being a live music venue, The Junction also puts on the odd club night

at the weekend. Fridays feed the worrying national trend for people who wish to dress up in seventies and eighties clobber. Abba to A-ha and the obligatory 'YMCA' all night long. Saturdays see a rotation of nights including house, R'n'B, jungle and garage. All are massively popular, but none can compete with the 'Dot Cotton Club' at the end of the month. Predominantly gay and lesbian, but all are welcome providing you dress up for the occasion.

Kambar
1 Wheeler Street (01223) 357503
Once upon a time, this was Route 66. Now it's less of a club, and more of a 'venue', which is slightly misleading seeing as it's the size of a shoe-box, and just as dark. Edging towards mock-Tudor, at least Shakespeare would have felt at home, as does suburbia, every time it hires it out for a party. Promoters fill in the gaps with nights ranging from D'n'B to the only true indie night in the city. The bar's always busy but they'll whisk the change out of your pocket in one fell swoop. Get drunk elsewhere, get in and get dancing the booze-fuelled boogaloo.

Life
22 Sidney Street (01223) 324600
Choose Life, well maybe at least once. Formerly the Chicago Rock Café, and nothing can be quite as crap as that place was. Unfortunately a refurb and new name hasn't shaken off the old regulars. With enough divorcees to start a dating

Hot tip

agency, at least if you're under the age of forty you're guaranteed a pull. The middle-aged brigade aren't the sort of punters the owners are aiming at, but they're lumbered with them now. At least they're loyal, but then again, so are dogs. It's an old adage that "Life is sweet", as is "Life is shit". I'm with the latter, at least in here.

Po Na Na Souk Bar
7a Jesus Lane (01223) 323880

When this place arrived in 1995 it was like an oasis in a desert, and it's still the best venue in town. The mixed music policy attracts a broad section of Cambridge folk, strutting their stuff to some fine house, hip hop, garage and Latino vibes. The Monday salsa night even allows you to brush up your dance moves with lessons. Whilst any budding superstar DJs can enter Wednesdays competition to become a Po Na Na in-house DJ. The layout allows you to dance yourself stupid, or chill out and chat to your mates in the quieter sections. Situated below Pizza Express, you'll be bolting your calzone, to get down here before it fills up, and trust me – it always does.

Toxic 8
1-6 Corn Exchange Street (01223) 477900

Finally the long overdue arrival of a city centre club, right next door to Lion Yard. Walk through the door and be prepared for an out of this world experience – in décor at least. The interior lies somewhere between a Flash Gordon and Alien film set, nicely rounded off with bright pink and cyan everywhere you look. Three floors to choose from, the top floor being the members area, with a lift to transport you between levels. Proving very popular with the students who are suitably impressed with the cocktail selection and a series of moving dance floors that vibrate in time with the beats. To be fair it all looks like a bad trip, but it's a cracking night out if you're in the right company. Pumping house and garage is the usual soundtrack, but midweek still caters for the cheesy tune lovers amongst you. Intoxicating indeed.

RIZLA+ It's what you make of it.

The Fez Club

15 Market Passage
(01223) 519224
thefezclub@cambridgecity.fsnet.co.uk

7a Jesus Lane
(01223) 323880
ponana@cambridgecity.freeserve.co.uk

Bring a copy of the book down, and take advantage of each of the following deals

- ☐ Free entry to Fez Club Mon - Thurs before 10.30pm
- ☐ A Happy Hour cocktail for £2.50 before 11pm at the Fez Club
- ☐ Two jugs of cocktails for £15 at Po Na Na, all night Mon -Thurs, and before 10pm Fridays and Saturdays
- ☐ 20% off party bookings at Po Na Na

Club	Night/Music Genre	Cost
Fez Club	70s, 80s, 90s and recent stuff	Free b4 10pm, NUS after 10 £2, others £3.50 after 9
Fifth Avenue	Hustle – 70s, 80s and early 90s	£3.50 b4 10.30pm, £4 after
Po Na Na	Salsa De La Buena – Salsa with lessons 7-9pm	£5 with lesson, £4 Nus, after 9pm £1.50
Toxic 8	Adelante – house, RnB and 70s	NUS free b4 10pm, 1/2 price after: Others £4 b4 11pm, £5 after 11pm
Fez Club	Classic cheese	Free b4 9pm, £4 b4 10pm, £5 after. NUS half price
Fifth Avenue	Big Holy Noise – anything goes	£3 b4 10.30pm, £4 after
Life	APU Sudent night – you ask they play!	£2
Po Na Na	United Rhythmns of RnB	£1.50 all night
Toxic 8	Love Shack – 70s and 80s dance classics	£1 b4 10pm, £3 b4 11pm, £5 after 11pm. NUS half price
Fez Club	Deep House	Free b4 9.30pm, £3 b4 11pm, £5 after 11pm. NUS half price
Fifth Avenue	Flex – Garage, soul and RnB	£4 all night
Life	C.U. Sudent night – you ask they play!	£2
Po Na Na	Industry – US garage	Free entry to all those 'in the industry'
Toxic 8	Livewire – anything and everything	£2 b4 10pm, £3 b4 11pm, £5 after 11pm. NUS half price
Fez Club	Rubber Soul	Free b4 9pm, £3 b4 11pm, £5 after 11pm
Fifth Avenue	Hey You – Europop, house, garage	NUS free b4 10pm and £2.50 b4 11pm, others £5.50 all night
Life	DJ Jonny Kipper	£5
Po Na Na	Private party night available for booking	-
Toxic 8	Goldrush – dance hits and party cheese	£1 b4 10.30pm, £3 b4 11pm, £5 after 11pm
Fez Club	House	£3 b4 9.30pm, £5 b4 10.30pm, £7 after 10.30pm
Fifth Avenue	Moist – house and garage	£1 b4 10.30pm, £4 b4 11pm, £5 after 11pm
The Junction	Boogie Wonderland – 70s and 80s	£6 in advance, £7 on door
Life	Mainstream – favs from 1960 to now	£5
Po Na Na	Funk and rare groove alternate weeks	Free b4 9pm, £3 b4 10pm, £4 after 10pm
Toxic 8	Evolution – garage, dance and trance	£4 b4 10.30pm, £5 b4 11.30pm, £6 after 11pm
Fez Club	House	£6 b4 10pm, £8 after 10pm
Fifth Avenue	Reality – Dance anthems, uplifting house	£5 b4 10.30pm, £6 after
The Junction	Good Times – house (1st Sat of month)	£7.50 in advance, £8.50 on door
	Rubber Soul – RnB, soul	£6.50 in advance, £8.50 on door
	Warning – Jungle	£11 in advance, £13 on door
	Faster Pussycat – UK garage	£10 in advance, £12 on door
	Dot Cotton Club – (last Sat of month)	£6.50 in advance, £7.50 on door
Life	Mainstream – Favs from 1960 to now	£5
Po Na Na	Nights alternate: Garage/RnB/70s+80s	Free b4 9, £3 b4 10pm, £4 after 10pm
Toxic 8	X-Cite – dance anthems	£5 b4 10pm, £7 b4 11pm, £8 after 11pm

For more up-to-date reviews, previews and listings check

    www.rizla.com

clubs

cafés

www.itchycity.co.uk

Arts Picture House Café
St. Andrews Street (01223) 572929

What kind of sad excuse for a human goes to a cinema caff? Not me. Unless it's the APH, resplendent with chandeliers, and not a Barry Norman in sight. Even late showings see people arriving early (you're only allowed up if you're here to catch a movie) to sink into sofas, socialise and snore. It's so relaxing, last time I was here someone was visiting the Land of Nod. Probably dreaming they were Harrison Ford.

Auntie's
1 St. Mary's Passage (01223) 315641

A couple of egg and cress sandwiches and some scones? If paying over the odds for 'traditional' is your idea of titillation, then you'll love Auntie's. With a minimum charge, and waitresses decked out in frilly, white aprons, it's a shame the prices haven't remained stuck in the past. You won't get 'feet on the tables' relaxation here, but you will find a whole host of 'Gee, how quaint' Yanks. Let a place named after your mum's sister round them up, and choose somewhere cheaper yourself.

Café Metro
57 Hills Road (01223) 304304
Perfect a cosmopolitan air, pronounce your words with a slight lisp and emphasise the wrong letters in sentences. Cambridge welcomes foreign visitors with open wallets, none more so than Café Metro who have tried to bridge the gap across the Channel by catering for our continental neighbours. The rest of us can settle back to the whirring of ceiling fans and some foul smelling, French cigarette smoking. Failing that, drop any pretence of European chic, confirm your typical lad(ette) status, and opt for takeaway, and a discount. At the very least, your stomach will have a decent lining, setting you up nicely for yet another binge.

Cazimir
13 King Street (01223) 355156
A Polish café, that's making its presence known for being overflowing with warmth, and colossal cups that look like they're about to follow suit. Not that they serve your bog-standard PG brew – they're not that conventional. Speciality teas reign supreme alongside Polish pastries and sandwich fillings.

Clowns
54 King Street (01223) 355711/460453
Try and remove any sinister Stephen King clown images from your head before you set foot in this homage to the classic circus entertainer. If you've always fancied yourself as a bit of a canvas dauber, then you can add your efforts to the many other paintings of clowns which paper the walls. Most of them the efforts of kids from local primary schools but I'm sure they won't mind if you think you can do better. Cheap, very tasty Italian food served until the early evening, and a genuinely laid-back environment to read the paper, touch up your essay or chat with mates. Show your face more than a handful of times and you'll become the owner's new best friend.

Copper Kettle
4 King's Parade (01223) 365068
Prime location for ogling Kings College, the Cambridge equivalent of St. Paul's. A prime target for academics as thankfully the stalls are ideal for avoiding the mock-intelligent discussions, but it can be worth getting a view of the action, as occasionally it gets so heated that even the windows steam up. Alternatively join in and disagree, straight-faced, that pi always equals a number to infinity. Go on, it'll be funny. I honestly.

www.itchycambridge.co.uk

Indigo

8 St. Edwards Passage (01223) 368753

Kinda like Central Perk, but charging them £10,000 every time you put in an appearance might be a bit off, especially when they put whipped cream and marshmallows in your hot chocolate, and act as your home from home.

Martin's

4 Trumpington Street (01223) 361757
Popular with the Leys pupils to the point that all teachers are wise to the fact. Not that it took them Holmes-scale sleuthing to discover, because they all go there too. The best breakfasts in town are worth the discomfort of the grotty loos, uncomfortable seats and abrupt service that'd make Anne Robinson seem friendly. Compared to 'Eggs, chips, beans?' bellowed from behind a counter, even 'You are the weakest link. Goodbye' starts to look conversational.

Starbucks

Fitzroy Street (01223) 356823
18 Market Street (01223) 328574
2 Quayside (01223) 303445
Starbucks march towards world domination has certainly reached blitzkrieg status with three of the blighters to choose from. If you're a caffeine craving, non-smoker you'll soon be one of the converted. Market Street offers muted warmth and bustle, Quayside's best for simple, summer socialising and Fitzroy Street resembles more a bar than a cafe, but it's Caramel Macchiatos all the way so you can cross it off your pub crawl.

Tatties

11 Sussex Street (01223) 323399
Serving up student spuds, it seems nobody can get enough tea with their 'tatties'. It's always been popular, probably explaining why it's been around for so long, it's still one of the best places to kill an hour or ten. Stuffed full of like-minded folk who have nothing better to do with their Monday afternoons. The fashion police have left this place off their beat or to put it another way, when it comes to naming a place, regulars can definitely prove inspirational.

The Little Tea Room

No.1 All Saints Passage (01223) 366033
Overlooking All Saint's Garden, Saturdays sees the craft market setting

Access across the globe...
via your WAP

wap.itchycambridge.co.uk

up shop, making the tables in the window the best place for hassle-free browsing. Best in summer, when the courtyard fills up with outside drinking, but as it's only tea, it's never going to get out of hand. It's a good job too, they couldn't handle 'bull-in-a-china shop' behaviour inside, as there's too many tea pots for sale on the shelves to leave room for a decent right hook.

Internet cafés

CB1

32 Mill Road (01223) 576306
Combining techie with traditional. Is that possible? Apparently so, and judging by the number of people here, they think so too. Mind you, they've got more board games and books than computers so I'm still not wholly convinced. Great as a café and an entertaining way of passing the time. Chess connoisseurs compete, others book-browse while the ones with the PCs cyber chat with busty Belinda from Bermuda (who's probably really big Brian from Bolton).

CB2

5-7 Norfolk Street (01223) 508503
CB1's younger cousin. Same concept but with slightly glossier presentation. You'll find it at the back of the Grafton Centre.

Internet Exchange

St. Mary's Passage (01223) 327600
An internet café in the finest sense of the word, except there's no café. So, none of your coffee, croissants, and one PC – this lot have a whole host of machines available, and know their stuff. A help desk saves you from those 'gaze into space and pretend I know what I'm doing' moments, or is that just me? With a member's card offering discounts and nationwide benefits, you can even surf as you wait for your plane at Stansted Airport. Full of students, many of whom seem to be doing dissertations on porn.

www.itchycity.co.uk

The gay scene in town is comparatively smaller than some of its national counterparts, but don't worry, it's just as flamboyant. Tearing off Cambridge's otherwise conservative image, with almost as much enthusiasm as Madonna used to rip her clothes off. With one of the best gay nights outside of London, and a handbag sized selection of pubs, you can grab your straight friends and make them welcome, posing to your heart's content. And that, my pretties, is that. Not all 'Queer as Folk', but for a little university city, it's not that bad.

Pubs

Five Bells
**126-128 Newmarket Road
(01223) 314019**
Just arrived in town, or just 'stepped out'. Outside it looks truly uninviting, but you'll find a warm welcome from the regulars, whether you're one of the pret-

ty folk or just pretty average. The beer garden's fantastic for summer gossiping, and people frequently do, so keep your ears open. Twice a month you get the chance to dust off your hotpants and get glittered-up at the 'disco'. If you're a true exhibitionist you can sit at home polishing your PVC in preparation for the fetish night. It only takes place once every three months, but it's well worth the wait.

Fleur de Lys
73 Humberstone Road (01223) 356095

Gay friendly, it can't quite commit, but then I'm not one to argue with keeping an open mind. The views of Elizabeth Way Bridge and the petrol station are hardly awe-inspiring, fortunately there's enough inside to keep your eyes diverted from the world outside. Shy types may not feel at ease as it's all about getting involved with whatever's going on. Choose a team and take part in a mixture of quizzes, darts and pool, just make sure you pick the winning team. Losers don't live it down easily, and you'll be picked last next time, just like the football teams at school when you were just a wee slip of a thing. It makes me cringe just thinking about it.

Town and Gown
Pound Hill (01223) 353791

A tongue-in-cheek atmosphere where drinks flow by the cocktail load and you'll come across some flamboyant characters. This usually means a full to bursting pub at the weekend, but your tongue's unlikely to stay in your cheek, and it's even less likely you'll be going home alone. Music is the usual Steps anthems played loud and proud giving you the chance to practice your moves before you hit the clubs. Making an effort on your appearance is always appreciated, and you will more often than not be rewarded for your troubles.

Club Night

Dot Cotton Club
The Junction, Clifton Road
(01223) 511511

Dust off your glad rags, powder your nose, and pull on your cheek-chafing thong. Don't complain now. Straight-friendly doesn't detract from the fun, it just gives more opportunities for showing off. The best music this side of London, it's handbags all the way, and attracts a gaggle of out-of-towners. All Cambridge residents should feel it their duty to make our neighbours welcome, and there are few places more welcoming than the Dot Cotton Club. Still waiting for Nick to make an appearance though. I've always had a soft spot for his roguish charms.

shopping
www.itchycity.co.uk

Shopping Centres

Grafton Centre
46 Grafton Centre (01223) 316201
Restaurants and a cinema on the top floor while the ground floor's dedicated to burning some wonga in the chainey stores. There's also a multi-storey car park round the back, so that those blisters you've acquired on the way round won't rub more than is strictly necessary.

Lion Yard
St. Tibbs Row (01223) 350608
Previously home to many of Cambridge's numerous winos, and nothing more than a shortcut from the car park to Sidney Street, Lion Yard has had a much needed face lift. HMV takes pride of place, and the newly laid floor prevents any unnecessary broken bones, which was usually the case when wet. The toilets are still a disgrace though.

Department Stores

Debenhams
Grafton Centre (01223) 353525
Same stuff the U.K. over. Beauty products (male and female), gift ideas, home furnishings and clothing. You're never going to come out in an excited hot flush, but you're rarely going to be disappointed either.

Robert Sayle
**12-17 St. Andrews Street
(01223) 361292**
A Cambridge institution, so much a part of the town it might as well be put on

the map. Electrical goods, clothing, beauty counters, fabrics, clocks and china...the list goes on.

Markets

Cambridge Market
Market Square
Stalls are open six days a week, selling everything from potted Stilton to second-hand cycles and cashmere. Usual shop opening times.

All Saints Garden Art and Craft Market
Gold and silversmiths, ceramics, textiles and paintings to name a few. Only open Saturday 10am-5pm.

Clothes

Unisex Fashion

Cult Clothing
37 Sidney Street (01223) 315550
Independent shop, shifting street, skate and club wear. Jeans, skate pants, tops, bags and culty stuff in general.

Dogfish/Catfish
5 Green Street (01223) 368088
Jeans, streetwear, bags, shoes and accessories for cool 'kats' (and dogs). Dogfish (men's) labels include Stussy, Carhartt, Evisu while Catfish fits out the ladies with Stylelab, Stussy, Silas, Duffer, Diesel, G-Star and Hysteric Glamour.

Giulio
24-32 King Street (01223) 316100

Award-winning shop for those flash and loaded enough to splash out. Smart clothes, bags and shoes will convert even the scruffiest of style-haters. Men can choose from Nicole Farhi, Miu Miu, Hugo Boss, Maharishi, Stone Island and C.P. Company, to name just a few. More limited selection for women by Jil Sander, Prada, Gucci, Armani, Patrick Cox and Paul Smith.

Javelin
17 Green Street (01223) 327320
Smart new shop for guys and girls. Get your matching outfits from labels including Peter Worth, Firetrap, French Connection, Gas, O'Neill, Quiksilver and Urban Stone.

Mayhem
41 Sidney Street (01223) 322030
Street/surf/skate clothing, bags, hats, accessories and crazy gifts. Labels aplenty including Ring Spun, Rip Curl, Billabong, Naf Naf and Miss Sixty. They've also got their own label. Capitalist mayhem.

Vertical
72 King Street (01223) 305222
Cambridge's coolest skate shop. Clothing, boards, shoes and accessories for guys and gals. There are boards everywhere and they even sell graffiti paint, though it's solely for artistic purposes of course. Fly, Putsch, Mecca, Mo Fu, Attic and Supreme Being, along with all the usual skate brands bought mainly by people who know their Tony Hawks from their Tony Harts.

Women's Fashion

Blu Max
18 King Street (01223) 500710
Friendly, relaxed shop for designer-label addicts. D&G, Moschino, Versace, Valentino, Iceberg, Full Circle and new fashion darling, Roberto Cavalli.

Bowns
25 Magdalene Street (01223) 302000
Smart clothing for the suitably attired set, and the more discerning mature shopper.

East
62 Sidney Street (01223) 324577
Embroidered kimonos, silk scarves, jewellery and clothing spread across two floors. Pricey but unique, worth saving for and great for presents.

Hero
12 Green Street (01223) 328740
Glossy, glass fronted shop housing designer labels aplenty. The saviour of Cambridge's fashion scene, stocking clothes, bags and scarves. Names include Ghost, Shirin Guild and Cashmere Studio and scarves by Jo Gordon.

Hobbs
10 Trinity Street (01223) 361704
Conservative clothes for smart, more experienced (old) lady. Clothes, bags, shoes, all from their own label.

Troons
16 Kings Parade (01223) 360274
Directly opposite Kings College, it's pretty small with some unusual one-off pieces, such as suede patchwork skirts. Pretty hefty price tags so make sure you take your credit card.

Men's Fashion

Anthony
18 Trinity Street (01223) 360592
Quality menswear stockists, specialising in Eton shirts, Canali and Hugo Boss, and that's just for starters.

Blu Max
2 King Street (01223) 352668
Helpful assistants advise your choice of purchase from an array of designer labels including Henri Lloyd, Iceberg, D&G, Moschino, Versace and Valentino. Seek advice from your bank manager first.

Ede and Ravenscroft
71-72 Trumpington Street
(01223) 350048
Established way back in 1689, this is traditional gentleman's tailoring for wannabes and the real McCoy alike. Blazers, silk ties, suits, DJs etc.

Reeves
62-64 King Street (01223) 322301
Thomas Burberry, Lacoste, Valentino, Versace and Firetrap.

Second-hand Clothes

Alternative Clothing Sale
Fisher Hall
Practically a Cambridge institution, they've been running for so long. No particular pattern to when they're held (but at least once a month), you'll find out when you're handed a flyer in the street. With flared cords, Levis and cheap T-shirts, there's more tie-dye than Glastonbury.

TOP FIVE... Outside drinking
1. The Anchor
2. The Mill
3. Henry's
4. The Granta
5. The Boat House

Hive and Honeypot
Dales Brewery, Gwydir Street
(off Mill Road) (01223) 300269
Dress exchange open seven days a week. Clear out your clutter, but they won't accept ra-ra skirts (unless there's a revival), and pick up some bargains to boot. Car parking opposite for all those bags you're bound to have.

www.palenque.co.uk
29 Sidney Street, CAMBRIDGE
TEL: 01223 362651

Shoes

Dune
17 Market Street (01223) 303313
Classy chain for well-dressed, female feet.

Raw
7 Peas Hill (01223) 302306
Men's and women's shoes such as Acupuncture, Diesel, Vans and Etnies.

soletrader
37-38 Petty Cury (01223) 460260
Fine selection of footwear. The list is endless, but to name a few, there's Ted Baker, French Connection, Hugo Boss, Camel,

Buffalo and Timberland, for men and women. Trendy shoes and trainers without the hefty price tag.

Music

Andy's Records
29-33 Fitzroy Street (01223) 361038
Tapes, records, CDs for the mainstream masses and the 'specialists' amongst you. Stocking everything from trance, techno and house to rock, reggae and indie. Plus all the usual chart favourites.

Garon Records
70 King Street (01223) 362086
Classical, blues, world music and jazz, both new and second hand. Mainly CDs but they also do vinyl. The best bit? There's 10% off all cash purchases over £5.

Heffers Sound
19 Trinity Street (01223) 568562
Classical music dominates, but there's a smattering of jazz. Mainly CDs.

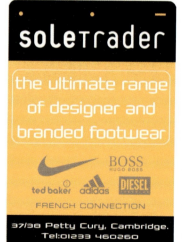

soletrader
the ultimate range of designer and branded footwear
NIKE · BOSS HUGO BOSS · ted baker · adidas · DIESEL · FRENCH CONNECTION
37/38 Petty Cury, Cambridge.
Tel:01233 460260

HMV
12-15 Lion Yard (01223) 319090
Huge store housing CDs, records, tapes and the odd MD. Commercial chart stuff with separate specialist areas from house to hip hop.

Jays Records
50 Burleigh Street (01223) 368089
Vinyl, tapes and CDs but they specialise in vinyl across indie, hip hop, RnB and dance.

MDC Classic Music
8 Rose Crescent (01223) 506526
Predominantly classical music, with a sprinkling of jazz and world music thrown in to keep the muso students happy. CDs only.

Parrot Records
93 King Street (01223) 312552
Probably the best place in town to buy your CDs with their extensive range of mid-priced albums, plus new releases around the £10 mark. Chart favourites alongside jazz, blues, indie and rock as well as a pretty decent dance selection.

Rhythm Syndicate Records
5 Cobble Yard, Napier Street
(01223) 323264/362212
All vinyl ranging across every area of dance music. A Cambridge resident for five years, loads of their business is now done through mail-order. Aspiring DJs are in good company as they flog their wares to some big name jocks including John Digweed, Danny Howells and Anthony Pappa

Streetwise Music
76 King Street (01223) 300496
Ten years old now, they were the first supplier of dance in the area, supplying Vigi of Big Bed Records, Marine Parade and TCR. With an online mail-order service supplying music worldwide which covers all the latest dance releases. Specialising in vinyl, they cover deep, tech, hard and progressive house, D'n'B and garage.

Gonwanaland

The best choice of Futon Sofabeds in Cambridge

◆

Designer Gifts

◆

Great Gadgets

◆

Tactile Textiles

◆

Kitchen & Bedroom Accessories

22 Mill Road Cambridge
01223 369050
&
32 Queen Street Haverhill
01440 713100

◆ futons ◆
◆ interiors ◆
◆ innovation ◆

V Shop
4 Bridge Street (01223) 363221
New release CDs, mainly chart singles and albums. Also stock DVDs.

Virgin Megastore
28 Grafton Centre (01223) 360333
V Shop's bigger brother, stocking a larger range of chart music and more specialised genres. Mainly CDs but some vinyl for latest dance releases.

Games

Electronics Boutique
3 Petty Cury (01223) 303262
A handful of second hand games and the usual range of newly released games though the prices are nothing to bash your joystick at.

Game
10 Lion Yard (01223) 366944
Huge store with an even bigger selection of all the usual suspects. Catch it before it burns a hole in the shopping centre roof, there's more neon than National Lampoon's Christmas Vacation.

Gametron Exchange
56 King Street (01223) 462825
New and second hand games from this small game worshipper's paradise.

Gifts

Botanicus
23 Petty Cury (01223) 354057
Lifestyle products with real value. Housed beneath the Botanicus' high ceil-

ings, there's everything from spices, teas, vinegars and bath oils, through to zinc and enamel objects of desire.

Breeze
34 Trinity Street (01223) 354403
Brand new independent shop, selling what are apparently known as interior home accessories. Basically, it sells table, glass and giftware, with the compulsory candles and door 'furniture'. Knobs to you and me.

Catherine Jones
9 Bridge Street (01223) 361596
Modern jewellery and original designs from designers such as Georg Jensen. Prices to suit any pocket, with ranges in silver, gold, platinum and other precious stones.

Chaps
15 Green Street (01223) 327262
Designer gifts for guys with a sense of humour. From cheeky board games to executive 'toys', it's the best place to pick up a present to look as if you care, even if you don't.

Gonwanaland
22 Mill Road (01223) 369050
A haven for unusual home and giftware stuff. From futons to beautiful leather beanbags. There's individually hand painted ceramics, quirky bottle openers and bathroom products. The list is endless, better to find out for yourself.

The Magic Joke Shop
29 Bridge Street (01223) 353003
The only place to equip yourself to attempt a challenge on Paul Daniels' dominance in the art of mixing comedy with magic.

Palenque
29 Sidney Street (01223) 362552
Mexican jewellery, gifts and funky mirrors all housed within a shiny shop. Perfect for the mythical man who has everything. The friendly staff are happy to help you in your search for that special something. Original designs and pocket-friendly prices.

Le Reve
6 Bene't Street (01223) 328111
Sexy lingerie for that special someone. And no, we're not talking crotchless. La Perla, Marie-Jo, Aubade, and the Queen's own Rigby and Peller. They've got an exclusive bridal underwear range, which is bound to make any man reconsider their views about marriage.

Other Cool Shops

Forbidden Planet
60 Burleigh Street (01223) 301666
Comics, toys, videos, models and science fiction books for all you warrior princesses and Trekkies out there. This is the place to find that wacky gift. Even the man who has everything is unlikely to own a full set of Buffy dolls. The force will be with you.

The Haunted Bookshop
9 St. Edwards Passage (01223) 312913
Terrifying titles to trap the victim of your affections. How can they not want to snuggle closer for protection after reading one of these books? Or maybe they'll just think you're a dodgy weirdo. Take your chances.

Talking T's
37 Bridge Street (01223) 302411
Design your own T-shirts to piss off your mates. They provide the stock, and you come up with the wacky slogan. They also sell Cambridge University crested items for Americans and geeks.

Waterstone's
6-7 Bridge Street (01223) 300123
22 Sidney Street (01223) 351688
The nice people at Waterstones have provided enough books to sate your thirst for knowledge and cafes to nourish you whilst you do so. From textbooks to trashy novels, maps to medieval literature, it's all here along with the full range of fabulous itchy guides for your delight and entertainment.

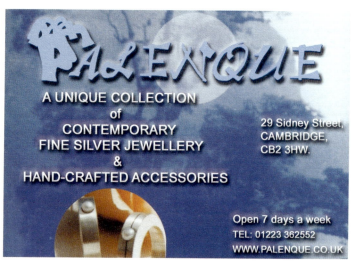

PALENQUE

A UNIQUE COLLECTION
of
CONTEMPORARY
FINE SILVER JEWELLERY
&
HAND-CRAFTED ACCESSORIES

29 Sidney Street,
CAMBRIDGE,
CB2 3HW.

Open 7 days a week
TEL: 01223 362552
WWW.PALENQUE.CO.UK

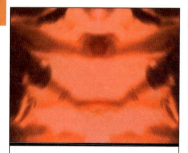

entertainment & tourism

www.itchycity.co.uk

Cinemas

Arts Picturehouse
38 St. Andrews Street (01223) 504444
Plush new cinema with its own café, and the usual soft drink and popcorn options to keep your energy levels up. Get pretentious with foreign-language films (fingers crossed for subtitles), fill up on your quota of latest releases, or go along for the after-pub night showings. Three screens.
B4 5pm Adult £3.50, NUS £3. After 5pm Adult £5.20 no NUS discount.

Warner Brothers Multiscreen
Grafton Centre (01223) 460442 (info)
Credit card bookings (01223) 460441
Eight-screen cinema to help those who've been running round the shops like headless chickens unwind. That said, the queues rival the M6, and they've generally just sold out when you reach the front, leaving you pretending to your mates that kiddies cartoons are the last word in cool. That's what the credit card booking line's for, and for the cinema it's an excuse to charge you extra for the privilege.

Theatres

ADC
Park Street (01223) 359547 (admin)
Box Office (01223) 503333
Used by amateur and professional dramatic companies. It's the headquarters for the University of Cambridge's Dramatic Club as well as playing host to fringe theatre productions throughout the summer.

Arts Theatre
Peas Hill (01223) 503333
Host to professional and amateur companies, from international tours to local pantomime. There's also opera, comedy, dance and drama productions as well as a restaurant and bar.

Cambridge Drama Centre
**Covent Garden (off Mill Road)
(01223) 322748**
When it's not catering to audiences of new theatre productions they hold weekend drama workshops.

Mumford Theatre
**Anglia Poly, Broad Street
(01223) 352932**
Productions by students, professional companies and amateur groups. Varied theatre, music, dance and operatic performances, staged on a regular basis.

Live Music Venues

The Boat Race
170 East Road (01223) 508533
There used to be a time when this was awash with up and coming bands. In 1994, a mono-browed group played here, with a surly attitude marking them out as destined for the local police cells or on the fast track to supernova heights. Unfortunately few bands of the calibre of Oasis have tread the boards since. Nowadays, it's mainly tribute bands and blues, but it's still the only place in town that has live music seven nights a week. Pop down on Sunday or Monday and you can get in for free.

Cambridge Corn Exchange
Wheeler Street (01223) 357851

Set in an impressive Victorian building, it's acoustically brilliant thanks to the high ceiling. There's more than enough space to swing hundreds of cats, but the only ones you'll find here are of the cool 'kat', human variety. Rock and pop groups, touring theatres and operas, comedy, ballet, full-scale orchestras and all night dance events are testament to the broad selection of entertainment available. Still primarily a gig venue, but don't opt for the upstairs seating. You can't stand up or drink beer, so get yourself down the front and work up a sweat.

TOP FIVE... Things to do
1. Punting
2. King's College
3. Fitzwilliam Museum
4. Drinking by the river
5. Dodge the cyclists

The Junction
Clifton Road (01223) 511511
Where all the little, 'big' bands play to a backdrop of plastic-glassed, beer-holding punters. In their time they've had the likes of Blur, Travis and The Manics playing here before moving onto the stadiums, and they're still attracting the best in alternative music. Due to smarten up its act with layout changes and a lick of paint, but it will all be lost on the indie kids.

Man on the Moon
Norfolk Street (01223) 360268
This place has had more name changes than an ex-con. Passing itself off as The Office for a while, before finally accepting that sometimes the original is still the best. Great on Saturdays when the bands are playing, but during the week it's dour, which even the beautiful barmaids can't change.

Portland Arms
129 Chesterton Road (01223) 357268
You wouldn't expect to find up and coming bands playing in the back room of what appears to be a naval-themed pub, but it is, and they do. Spit and sawdust, friendly, I practically live in this pub, but then I do live next door.

The Sophbeck Sessions
14 Tredgold Lane, Napier Street (01223) 569100
An underground club, that's primarily dedicated to jazz, with a smattering of blues thrown in for good measure. More subterranean than anarchic with a plush wine cellar theme, and an atmosphere as chilled as a polar bear on ice. It's easy to feel like a true Kerouacian hero listening to jazz 'til dawn (or eleven, in this case), but it needs to lose some of the 'old-skool' jazz musicians to appeal to the youngsters. Progressive freeform, anyone?

Snooker/Pool Halls

Frames
Coldhams Road (01223) 249661
Snooker £3.75 p/h, nine ball £5 p/h, small pool tables 50p a game.
Annual membership £10 per person.
Open seven days a week 12pm-11.30pm

you've tried this one...now try them all 17 other cities to indulge in

www.itchycambridge.co.uk

W.T.'s
39b Burleigh Street (01223) 350400
Eleven snooker tables, plus eight and nine ball tables.
Snooker £5.20 p/h, with NUS it's half price Mon-Fri until 7pm. Pool and nine ball run off meters at £1 for ten minutes. Lifetime membership (adults) £10, (NUS) £5. Members can sign in three guests for a £1 charge per person.
Mon/Tues open 24 hours, Wed-Sun 10.30am-11.30pm

Name and occupation?
Dominique, Alice, Melissa; students
Plenty of drinking time then. Favourite medicine cabinets?
Regal, Hogshead and Quay Bar
When you run out of beans on toast where do you blow the loan?
Pierre Victoire, Café Rouge
You'd rather be at a lecture than in?
5th Avenue or Life

Karting/Laser/Paintball

Kartsport UK
Royston Road, Caxton (01954) 718200
Groups: minimum 20 people £37.50 per person, if there's less than 20 you make up the difference, 40 people and over £35 per person. 'Arrive and drive' (indoor) £20 for half an hour (outdoor) £1 a minute, 15 minutes minimum.

Laserquest
**13-15 Bradwells Court
(01223) 302102**
Whilst 'corporate armies' are welcome, I'd take my chances on my own, but then I'm brave like that.
Non-members £3 (week), £3.50 (weekends), members and NUS £2.50 (weekdays and weekends). Membership £10 per year.
Open seven days a week, 10.30am-9pm

Survival Games
**Paint Chase House, Walpole Road
(01223) 567665**
Make Jane from accounts pay for that new tax code.
Full day £34, half day £27, two and a half hour session £16

Football

Cambridge United FC
**Abbey Stadium, Newmarket Road
(01223) 566500**
Tickets £7-£14
The U's have a less than illustrious history, and it would appear that little is going to change that in the future. It wasn't so long ago, in the days of Dion Dublin and Steve Claridge that United stood on the brink of the Premiership. It all went pear-shaped from that moment on, although manager Roy McFarland has brought some stability to the club who are firmly rooted in the middle of the Second

Division. Come on down to the Abbey and experience facilities you just don't see in the Premiership anymore.

Tourist

University Colleges

A day out in Cambridge wouldn't be right without some academia. Rather than strain your own mind, visit a place where others do. At least you can leave when the uniform grass quads or 'courts' (meant to encourage studious reflection) get a bit much. Many are open free of charge to visitors, but there are some who've gone all mercenary, and will charge you for the privilege. Here's a selection of the best.

Open all year except 23 Dec-3 Jan, and Easter term, 24 April-25 June.

Gonville and Caius
Trinity Street (01223) 332400
Pronounced Gonville and 'keys', there's medical tradition aplenty, as a former student unlocked the secret of how blood circulation works. Walk through the three gates, symbols of the students' academic path – Humility, Virtue and Honour. May the force be with you.

King's College
King's Parade (01223) 331100

Cambridge's most famous college and chapel. Its choir attracts visitors throughout the year, but none more so than Christmas Eve's Midnight Mass. Services are conducted by candlelight. Henry VI founded the college but the War of the Roses and his subsequent murder left the site empty for three hundred years. Mind you, he did lay the foundation stone and detailed arrangements in his will, leaving all the hard work to other people. It's a pretty impressive memorial, even now, so few would disagree that it was worth it.

Magdalene College
Magdalene Street (01223) 332100
Pronounced 'Maudlin', the Pepys building stands in the second court, housing 3,000 volumes from Samuel Pepys' library, including his famous diary. No shelf-shoplifting allowed here though, he insisted that no books should be added or removed from it. And the good people of Magdalene do as they're told, even posthumously.

Peterhouse
Trumpington Street (01223) 338200
Worth a visit, if only because it's the oldest of all the colleges dating from 1284. The hall's the only thing to have survived the thirteenth century, but that doesn't prevent an influx of inquisitive visitors passing through.

the Great Gate. It wasn't sharp enough to stop students removing his sceptre and replacing it with a chair leg, though, was it? One of the traditions is trying to run around The Great Court whilst the clock strikes twelve (remember Chariots of Fire?). It repeats the chimes twice. Maybe it's the Trinity College water or the fact they're just wacky students.

Queens' College
Queens' Lane (01223) 335511
Famous for the involvement of two queens – Margaret of Anjou and Elizabeth of Woodville – it's home to Erasmus' Tower. He lived and worked here between 1510 and 1514, with only his denounced 'heretical' tomes for company. The wooden Mathematical Bridge is also worth a look, supposedly originally constructed without bolts, until it unsurprisingly fell down. They've definitely put some in now though.

Trinity College
Trinity Lane (01223) 332500
Having worked his way through numerous wives, Henry VIII still managed to fit something else in before his death, merging two colleges to found Trinity. His statue keeps an eye on the proceedings from

Cambridge University Botanic Garden
Bateman Street (01223) 336265
Coming up close behind Kew Gardens in importance, it covers over 40 acres. Some of it's not for public visits, but research purposes – botanists take plants and flowers seriously. Greenhouses prevent the more exotic from getting frostbite. Alan Titchmarsh's wet dream.
Mar-Sept 10-6, Feb & Oct 10-5, Nov-Jan 10-4
Adults £2, free admission Wed 10-12

Museums

Cambridge University Collection of Air Photography
The Mond Laboratory, Free School Lane (01223) 334578
Over 400,000 air photographs, showing

how the landscape and human activity has changed in the local area. Look at The Fens and you'll see nothing has changed, even the people.
Free admission.
Mon-Thurs 9am-1pm, 2pm-5pm, Fri 'til 4pm

Cambridge University Museum of Classical Archaeology
Sidgwick Avenue (01223) 335153
Contains one of the largest collections of Greek and Roman sculpture plaster casts in the world. Over 600 pieces to root through, and every one as exciting as the other.
Free admission.
Mon-Fri 9am-5pm

Cambridge Museum of Technology
Cheddars Lane (01223) 368650
The building itself used to be a Victorian sewage-pumping station. Steam is produced by a hand-fired, Babcock & Wilcox boiler. Allegedly, the oldest land-based boiler still being steamed regularly. When it's steaming, the admission charge is higher. You might want to get steaming to enjoy it more.
Open first Sun of each month 2pm-5pm, and every Sun from Easter-November.

Cambridge University Museum of Zoology
Downing Street (01223) 336650
Exotic birds, mammal skeletons, corals and fossils. A bit like a visit to your local retirement home then. Some items were donated by Charles Darwin from his voyage on the Beagle.
Free admission.
Open Mon-Fri 2pm-4.45pm (term-time), Mon-Fri 10am-1pm (out of term)

Fitzwilliam Museum
Trumpington Street (01223) 332900
With a mosaic and marble foyer designed by E.M. Barry, it was one of Britain's first public art galleries. The art it now houses ranges from early Italian to the contemporary. Also displaying Egyptian, Greek, Roman and West Asiatic antiquities, along with musical and literary manuscripts, rare books, armour, ceramics, coins, medals and textiles, and that's just for starters.
Free admission
Tues-Sat 10am-5pm, Sun 2.15pm-5pm, guided tours Sunday at 2.30pm

Kettles Yard
Northampton Street (01223) 352124
Previously the home of Jim and Helen Ede, in 1966 it was given over to Cambridge University, and remains untouched. You can wander around taking in their collections of early twentieth-century paintings and sculptures.

Free admission.
House: Easter-August, Tues-Sun 2-4pm
Gallery: Tues-Sun 11.30am-5pm

Scott Polar Research Institute
Lensfield Road (01223) 336540
Founded in 1920 as a memorial to Robert Scott and his companions who died in 1912 on their way back from the South Pole. It's the most important polar library and archive in the world. Displays include diaries, clothing, photographs, relics, letters, watercolours and drawings.
Free admission.
Mon-Sat 2.30pm-4pm

Sedgwick Museum of Geology
Downing Street (01223) 333456
Houses the oldest, intact geological collection in Britain. Rocking.
Free admission.
Mon-Fri 9am-1pm, 2pm-5pm, Sat 10am-1pm

Art Galleries

Broughton House
98 King Street (01223) 314960
Exhibition gallery showing contemporary art by British and international artists.
Free admission
Tues-Sat 10.30am-5.30pm

Cambridge Contemporary Art Galleries
6 Trinity Street (01223) 324222
Commercial gallery displaying sculptures, ceramics and textiles.
Free admission
Mon-Sat 9am-5.30pm

Cambridge Darkroom
Dales Brewery, Gwydir Street (01223) 566725
Displaying touring exhibitions of photographs. Darkroom classes and facilities available. Exhibitions include workshops, discussion groups and videos.
Free admission
Tues-Sun 12pm-5pm

Conservatory Gallery
6 Hills Avenue (01223) 211311
Paintings and wall hangings produced by over fifty of East Anglia's leading artists.
Free admission
Sat 10am-5pm, and first Sunday of every month

Gallery 96
96 King Street (01223) 507725
Exhibition gallery with each one running for about three weeks. The diversity of artists includes narrative, figurative, abstract, literary and Cambridge themes. Looking just outside the local area they always welcome visits from new artists. Featured artists include Cynthia Howell and Julia Hesseltine.
Free admission
Tues-Sat 10am-4.30pm with relaxed preview showings early evening.

Lawson Gallery
7-8 King's Parade (01223) 313970
Exhibition and commercial gallery selling antique prints and maps.
Free admission
Mon-Sat 9.30am-5.30pm

Primavera
10 King's Parade (01223) 357708
Contemporary paintings, ceramics, wood and craft work, available to purchase.
Free admission
Mon-Sat 9.30am-5.30pm

Sebastian Pearson
3 Pembroke Street (01223) 323999
1840-1940 British watercolours and oil paintings and 20th century British prints, including etchings and lithographs.
Free admission
Mon-Sat 10.30am-5pm

Out of Cambridge

American War Cemetery
Madingley Road, Coton (01954) 210350
A corner of Cambridgeshire that shall forever belong to America. Dedicated to the American servicemen who gave their lives during World War Two, the majority of whom were based in the area. 3812 headstones, and the 427 feet Tablets of The Missing inscribed with the names of 5126 soldiers missing in action. A truly humbling experience. Come here to remind yourself just how lucky you are.

Anglesey Abbey
Lode, Cambridge (01223) 811200
Lord Fairhaven's home, but yours for a day along with the hundreds of other visitors. If good old H_2O's your thing, then you'll be in liquid paradise with the working water mill. Antique Roadshow fanatics should check out the real thing, with the paintings and antiques on display in the Abbey. The gardens come complete with statues, and they're not your suburban, gnome variety either.
25 Mar-22 Oct, Wed-Sun 10.30am-5.30pm, Gardens and Mill open daily 3 Jul-17 Sep
Winter Walk 26 Oct-23 Dec, 10.30am-dusk.
Adults (Abbey & gardens) £6.10, Adults (gardens only) £3.75, Adults (Winter walk) £3

Audley End House
Saffron Walden (01799) 522842
The house is displayed in all its 18th and

THE INDEPENDENT ON SUNDAY   The best coverage of news & sport

19th century splendour, and it's not looking bad for its age. It's been taken under the National Trust's wing, which literally translated means more guide books and tours than there are 'antiquated objects'. Expect to see coach loads of pensioners, home-made sarnies and coffee flasks in hand. It's also a fine place for drunken teenagers to run around in the gardens at night. 'Capability' Brown designed the gardens, and very capably as well.

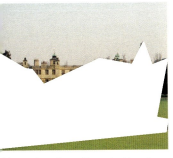

House 1pm-6pm, Grounds 11am-6pm, 10am-3pm (Oct only)
House and grounds: Adults £6.50, Concs £4.90, Grounds only: Adults £4.50, Concs £3.40

Chilford Hall Vineyard
Balsham Road, Linton (01223) 892641
The secrets of fine wine revealed. So now you know the difference between Blue Nun and Beaujolais, without having to drink a bucket of the stuff and wait for the resulting hangover.
Open seven days a week, from Good Friday-1 Nov, 11am-5pm
Free entry but guided tours £4.50.

Duxford Imperial War Museum
Duxford, 5 minutes south down M11 Junction 10
(01223) 835000
Biplanes, Spitfires, Concorde and Gulf War jets are just some of the 150 historic aircraft on show. Biggles enthusiasts roam in all their flying jacketed glory, walking through battlefield scenes with tanks and artillery on display. Regular air shows draw in the crowds from even further afield as well as plenty of cheapskates watching from afar to avoid the entrance fee. If you can't be bothered to wait, the American Air Museum presents their aircraft suspended as though in mid-flight. You'll look pretty stupid if you 'ooh' and 'aah' here, even if you are trying to create your own show.
Open seven days a week, all year (except 24-26 Dec), 10am-6pm in summer, 10am-4pm in winter
Adults £7.40, Concs £3.70

Ely
20 minute drive north of Cambridge, off A10
Stuck in the heart of pure Fenland country, what's the big deal? Well, if you're travelling there by train or car, there's one for a start. There was a time when you'd have been travelling by boat and avoiding numerous eels. It used to be an isle before the Fens were drained, and the surrounding water was seething with the slippery things. Now it's home to the incredibly impressive Ely Cathedral, a few quiet, traditional boozers and not much else.

body

www.itchycity.co.uk

Hairdressers

Unisex

Directors
8-9 Green Street (01223) 311393/1
Smart and sleek salon, for those who don't mind paying a bit more to come out looking as such.
Mon/Tues/Fri 9am-6pm, Wed/Thurs 9am-8pm, Sat 8am-5pm
20% NUS discount Mon-Thurs.
Men £27/Women from £30

Essensuals
1-2 Peas Hill (01223) 467667
With the mother company being Toni & Guy, you pretty much know what to expect. Don't be put off by the scary-looking photographs in the window. They'll tailor it to what you want. Apparently.
Mon 10am-7pm, Tues/Wed 10am-9pm, Thurs/Fri 10am-7pm, Sat 9am-5pm
15% NUS discount Mon-Wed 9am-5pm
Men £24/Women £29

Philip Helliar
9 Bene't Street (01223) 355943
Small salon, offering attentive scissor service.
Mon-Fri 9am-4.30pm, Sat 9am-3.30pm
Men £16.50/Women £27.50

Scruffs
76 Mill Road (01223) 367672
First name-friendly, family-run salon with qualifications galore, and staff who'll listen to what you want, rather than tell you what they think (unless you ask). Included in the price of your cut are complimentary consultations, treatment shampoos and conditioners, shiatsu massage with your hair wash and a choice of refreshments from the menu. No wonder then that customers always come back, and bring their friends. It's something of a rarity for clients to bring presents with them at Christmas, but it happens here. Then again, this is a pretty special place.
Mon/Fri/Sat 8am-6pm, Tues-Thurs 8am-8pm
NUS discount
Men £23/ Women £25

Listed in the TOP 50 hairdressers in Great Britain

scruffs

01223 367672
76 Mill Road Cambridge CB1 2AS
www.scruffs.co.uk

Toni & Guy
10 Bridge Street (01223) 462662
Bustling salon, great for when you're in a rush but not if you want to relax and appreciate all that money you're spending. They'll snip a few strands off in an 'artistic' way, before getting your coat with Mansell-like speed, and beckoning you to their make-up range on your way out.
Mon/Tues/Fri/Sat 9am-6pm, Wed/Thurs 9am-9pm
Men £25/Women £30

Gents Barbers

The Barber Shop
7 The Broadway (01223) 410439
Mon-Thurs 8.30am-6pm, Fri 8.30am-7pm, Sat 8.30am-5.30pm
Shampoo and cut £9.75

Mr. Polito's
4 Silver Street (01223) 369622
Mon-Fri 8.30am-5.30pm, Sat 8.30am-4.30pm
Shampoo and cut £12.50

Tempo
74 King Street (01223) 369119
Mon-Fri 9am-6pm, Sat 9am-5pm
Dry cut £8/£7 NUS

Health Clubs

Atrium Club
64 Newmarket Road (01223) 522522
Gym, free weights, jacuzzi, steam room, sauna and crêche.
Mon-Fri 6.30am-10pm, Sat/Sun 8am-5pm
Day pass and membership prices available on request.

Club Moativation
Granta Place, Mill Lane (01223) 259989
Swimming pool, jacuzzi, steam room, sauna, gym and beauty salon.
Mon-Fri 7am-10pm, Sat/Sun 7.30am-9pm
Day pass £25, mem. prices on request.

Glassworks
**Halfmoon Yard, Quayside
(01223) 305060**
Stylish-looking gym including water resistance rowing machines and free weights section, aerobics studio with adjustable lighting, separate health and juice bar, sauna, steam room, Aveda treatment rooms and retail products plus TVs to watch as you work up a sweat. New sunken jacuzzi with riverside views.
Mon-Fri 7am-9.30pm, Sat/Sun 9am-7pm
Joining fee: £150-£250.
Membership – Full: £610 (annual) £56.50 (monthly). Off peak: £480(annual), £44.50 (monthly). Guest day passes £15 peak, £10 off peak.

Leisure Centres

Kelsey Kerridge Sports Hall
Queen Anne Terrace (01223) 462226
Squash, badminton, table tennis, five-a-side football, volleyball and a climbing wall.

YMCA
Gonville Place (01223) 356998
Aerobics classes including Step and Tae Bo, and a gym with specialist disability machines.

Tattooists

Moving Pictures
396 Mill Road (01223) 241485
Mon-Sat 10.30am-5pm
Minimum charge £15

Mystic Ink
177 Victoria Road (01223) 361155
Tues-Sat 10am-6pm
Prices start from £15

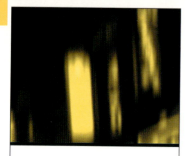

Pizzas & Burgers

A.B.C
15 The Broadway, Mill Road
(01223) 244538

Bosphorus
54 Mill Road (01223) 311579

Domino's Pizza
27 Hills Road (01223) 355155

Fagito
6 Mill Road (01223) 366070

Flying Pizza
Barnwell Drive (01223) 244874/5

The Gardenia
Rose Crescent (01223) 566826

Original Pizza Co.
22 Cheddars Lane (01223) 462308

Perfect Pizza
178 Mill Road (01223) 410800

Pizza Wheels
59 Hills Road (01223) 360444/366222

Indian/Asian

Curry Fast
2b Victoria Avenue (01223) 322233

Curry Garden
60 Hills Road (01223) 242492/411885

Curry & Pizza
5b High Street, Milton
(01223) 861948/505177

Kismet
71 Catherine Street (01223) 410225

Moghul Tandoori
182 Sturton Street
(01223) 352789/353788

Shahi Balti
106 Cherry Hinton Road
(01223) 247501

Oriental

Dragon
60 Mill Road (01223) 506800

Golden Wok
191 Histon Road (01223) 350688

Hong Kong House
8 Milton Road (01223) 369436

Hong Kong Takeaway
24a&b Chesterton Road
(01223) 354094

Lotus House
166 Mill Road (01223) 243492

Sushi Express Co.
50 Hills Road (01223) 516016

TOP FIVE
Watch the footie
1. CC's Sports Bar
2. Hogshead
3. King Street Run
4. Quinn's
5. The Graduate

Fish'n'Chips

Golden Valley
88 Campkin Road (01223) 423288

Jack's
202 Cherry Hinton Road
(01223) 247612

Sang's
140 Wulfstan Road (01223) 248722

Chicken

City Takeaway
82 Cherry Hinton Road
(01223) 244149

KFC
174 East Road (01223) 321034

cheap eats

www.itchycambridge.co.uk

getting about, accommodation & map

www.itchycity.co.uk

Taxi

3 A's	(01223) 30130
A1	(01223) 525555
Abba	(01223) 322322

Private Hire

Academy	0800 191022
Airport Cars	(01954) 782822
Atlantic	(01223) 510377
Alpha	(01954) 267444
Big Car Co.	(01223) 839888
Camtax	(01223) 313131
Falcon 5 Star	(01223) 414999
Intercity	(01223) 312233
Lima	(01223) 212122
Panther	(01223) 715715
Regency	(01223) 311388
National Express	08705 808080
Cambridge Coaches	(01223) 423900
Jetlink	08705 757747
Park and Ride	0870 6082608
Cambus	(01223) 423578

Bike Hire

The Bikeman	0850 814186
Geoff's	(01223) 365629

Trains

National Rail Enquiries	08457 484950
Virgin Trains	08457 222333

Planes

Cambridge Airport	(01223) 373737
Stansted Airport	(01279) 680500

Car Hire

Avis..................................(01223) 212551
Budget ....(01223) 323838
Enterprise ....(01223) 368400
Hertz................................(01223) 416634

Accommodation

Price for one night, single room with breakfast.

Expensive

Cambridge Garden House Moat House
Granta Place, Mill Lane (01223) 259988
From £125 (week), £81 (weekend) including use of Club Moativation

Crowne Plaza
Downing Street (01223) 464466
£179 (week) £129 (weekend) excluding breakfast. Breakfast £12.50

Gonville Hotel
Gonville Place (01223) 366611
£95 excluding breakfast. Breakfast £9.50

University Arms
Regent Street (01223) 351241
£115 (week & weekend)

Mid Priced

Cam Guest House
17 Elizabeth Way (01223) 354512
£30 (week & weekend)

Cristina's
47 St. Andrew's Street (01223) 365855
£30 (week & weekend). Doubles only.

Southampton
7 Elizabeth Way (01223) 357780
£40 (week & weekend)

Warkworth House
Warkworth Terrace (01223) 363682
£30 (week & weekend)

Budget

Ashtrees
128 Perne Road (01223) 411233
£20 (week & weekend)

El Shaddai
41 Warkworth Street (01223) 327978
£25 (week & weekend)

Hills Guest House
157 Hills Road (01223) 214216
£33 (week & weekend)

YMCA
Queen Anne House, Gonville Place (01223) 356998
£23 (week & weekend)

Tourist Information
The Old Library, Wheeler Street (01223) 322640

index

Listings	Page Grid No. Ref.
Accommodation	73
ADC	56 D3
Air Photography Collection	10 C2
All Bar One	61 D4
All Saints Craft Market	18 E4
Alma, The	47 D3
Alternative Clothing Sale	49 E4
American War Cemetery	64
Anchor,The	22 D4
Andy's Records	50 G3
Anglesey Abbey	64
Anthony	49 D3
Archaeology Museum	62 B5
Art Galleries	65
Arts Picture House Café	40 E4
Arts Picturehouse	56 E4
Arts Theatre	57 D4
Audley End House	64
Auntie's	8 D3
Bar 8	18 E4
Bar Moosh	19 G6
Baron of Beef	23 D2
Bath House	23 D4
Blu Max	48/49 E3
Boat House, The	23 E1
Boat Race, The	57 G3
Botanic Garden	61 F6
Botanicus	52 E3
Bowns	48 C2
Breeze	53 D3
Broughton House	63 E3
Browns	19 E5
Bun Shop, The	7 E5
Burleigh Arms	24 H3
Café Metro	41 F5
Café Rouge	8 D2
Café Uno	11 D2
Cambridge Blue	24
Cambridge Curry Centre	10 C2
Cambridge Darkroom	63 H5
Cambridge Drama Centre	47 D3
Cambridge FC	25 C2
Cambridge Market	24 E4
Castle Inn	23 D2
Castle, The	41 E3
Catherine Jones	43 G4
Cazimir	43 H4
CB1	20
CB2	
CC's Sports Bar	
Champion of the Thames	25 E3
Chaps	53 D3
Charlie Chan	
Chato	14 F4
Chilford Hall Vineyard	65
Chili's	
Chopsticks	6 H3
Cinemas	14 C2
Clowns	56
Coach and Horses	41 E3
Conservatory Gallery	63 G6
Contemporary Art Galleries	
Copper Kettle	63 D3
Corn Exchange	41 D4
Cricketers, The	57 D4
Cult Clothing	47 D3
Curry Mahal	63 E3
Debenhams	
Devonshire Arms	
Dogfish/Catfish	47 D3
Dojo Noodle Bar	16 D4
Dome, The	
Don Pasquale	8 D2
Dune	11 D2
Duxford Imperial War Museum	24
East	
Ede and Ravenscroft	
Efes	57 H5
Ely	65
Empress, The	
Fez Club	34 D3
Fifth Avenue	
Fitzwilliam Museum	62 D4
Fleur de Lys	
Football	
Footlights	25 E3
Forbidden Planet	53 D3
Fort St. George	27 F4
Fountain Inn, The	58
Frames	27 G4
Free Press	
Gainsborough	16 D2
Gallery 96	52 E4
Game	57 C2
Garfunkel's	
Garon Records	50 E3
Giulio	
Globe, The	
Gonville and Caius	60 D3
Gonwanaland	41 D4
Graduate, The	57 D4
Grafton Centre	25 G4
Granta, The	47 D3
Green Man	28
Gulshan; The Ha Ha @ The Blue Boar	10 F5
	46 G3
	20 D3
Hairdressers	66
Haunted Bookshop	54 D4
Health Clubs	61 D5
Heffers Sound	58
Henry's	50 D3
Hero	20 D2
Hive and Honeypot	49 H5
HMV	48 E3
Hobbs	49 D3
Hobbs Pavilion	58
Hogshead	8 F4
India House	28 F4
Indigo	10 C5
Internet Cafés	42 D4
Internet Exchange	26
Javelin	43 D3
Jays Records	34 E4
Junction, The	62 E5
Junction, The	
Kambar	45 H2
Karting	59
Kartsport UK	6 G3
Kettles Yard	54 E3
King Street Run	27 F4
King's College	
La Margherita	
La Mimosa	27 G4
Lawson Gallery	63 E3
Le Reve	52 E4
Leisure Centres	68
Life	43 H5
Lion Yard	50 E3
Little Tea Room	47 D3
Live and Let Live	27 G6
Live Music	29 H5
Loch Fyne	57
Locomotive, The	28 E1
Magdalene College	60 C2
Magic Joke Shop	28 C5
Man on the Moon	58 H4
Martin's	42 D5
Mayhem	38 D2
Maypole, The	
MDC Classic Music	51 E3
Michel's Brasserie	9 C2
Midsummer House	9 E2
Mill, The	30 D4
Mitre, The	30 D4
Mumford Theatre	57 G4
Museums	61
No. 1 King's Parade	8 D4
Old Orleans	7 C4
Out of Cambridge	64
Paintball	59
Palenque	53 D3
Parrot Records	51 E3
Peking Restaurant	14 G3
Peterhouse	61 D5
Pickerel Inn, The	30 C2
Pierre Victoire	10 F5
Pizza Express	13 D3/E4
Po Na Na	37 D3
Portland Arms	58 F1
Primavera	
Quay Bar	21 D2
Queen's College	61 D4
Quinn's	30 E4
Rainbow	15 D4
Rat and Parrot 2	1E E2
Raw	50 D4
Reeves	49 E3
Regal, The	31 E4
Rhythm Syndicate	
Records	51 G3
Robert Sayle	46 E4
Rock, The	31
Rupert Brooke	32
Sala Thong	
Salsbury Arms, The	32 H6
Scott Institute	57
Sedgwick Museum of Geology	29 G4
Shalimar,The	53 D2
Snooker/Pool	58
soletrader	50 D3
Sophbeck Sessions,The	
Spread Eagle	58 G3
Square and Compasses	32 F5
St. Radegund	33
Starbucks	23 F3
Streetwise Music	62 G3,D2
Survival Games	51 E3
Takeaway	59
Talking T's	70
Tatties	54 D2
Tattooists	42 E3
Technology Museum	68
Thai Regent	62 D4
Theatres	56
Town and Gown	45
Toxic 8	37 E4
Tram Depot,The	33 G4
Trattoria Pasta Fresca	
Travel	14 G4
Trinity College	72
Troons	61 D3
22 Chesterton Rd	49 D4
University Colleges	7 E1
V Shop	60
Venue	52 D2
Vaults	17 D3
Vertical	17/21 F5
Virgin Megastore	48 E3
Warner Bros.	52 E3
Waterstone's	59 G3
Wrestlers, The	56 H3
WT's	54 D2/D3
Yippee	33
Zoology Museum	17 E3
	62 E4

www.itchycambridge.co.uk